PUJOL

GUITAR SCHOOL

To the memory of

Francisco Tárrega

spiritual phoenix of the guitar.

In homage with gratitude and admiration.

EMILIO PUJOL

Guitar School

A Theoretical=Practical Method
✤ for the Guitar ✤

Based on the Principles
of Francisco Tárrega

---

* Book Three *

PREFACE BY MANUEL DE FALLA
TRANSLATED AND EDITED
BY PETER SEGAL

Editions Orphée, Columbus

Editions Orphée, Inc.
P.O. Box 21291
Columbus, OH, 43221

Library of Congress Catalogue Card Number: 82-64565

Printed in the United States of America

98 97 95 94 93 92 91 5 4 3 2 1

Published September 1st 1991

Order N° RTFT-2

Designed by Matanya Ophee
Music engraved by Peter Segal, using Score 3.0 software

Library of Congress Cataloging-in-Publication Data
(Revised for vol. 3)

Pujol, Emilio, 1886
Guitar school.

Errata slip attached to 1st prelim. page of bk. 1-2.
Includes bibliographical references.
Contents: Books one & two / Translated by Brian
Jeffery ; edited by Matanya Ophee – Book three /
translated and edited by Peter Segal.
    1. Guitar—Methods. I. Tárrega, Francisco,
1852-1909. II. Falla, Manuel de, 1876-1946.
III. Jeffery, Brian. IV. Ophee, Matanya. V. Segal, Peter, 1949– . VI. Title.
MT582.P8413   1983   82-84565

ISBN 0-936186-07-0 (bk. 1-2)

ISBN 0-936186-57-7 (bk. 3)

TO EMILIO PUJOL

My dear friend:

Would that I were a Llobet or a Segovia, so that I might speak as I should about your Método de Guitarra, *and so that I might thus reciprocate the warmth with which you honor me by asking me for some words of introduction. But what could I add to the brilliant practical and theoretical teaching which we all owe to you? If there is anything I can say, it is only to render homage to this instrument, which has always occupied pride of place in the resonant halls and homes of Spain, and whose history is so often bound up with our own, indeed, with the whole history of European music.*

This admirable instrument, as sober as it is rich, sometimes roughly yet sometimes sweetly masters the soul. Through the centuries it has taken up into itself the values of noble instruments which have passed away, has taken those values into itself without losing its own character which it owes, in its origins, to the people itself.

One must acknowledge that the guitar, of all stringed instruments with a fingerboard, is the most complete and the richest in its harmonic and polyphonic possibilities. And more, the history of music itself shows us its magnificent influence as a means of transmitting throughout Europe the essence of the musical resonance of Spain. With what emotion do we find its clear echo in Scarlatti, in Glinka and his disciples, in Debussy and Ravel!

In our own music, which through the ages has owed so much to the guitar, we will only cite as a recent example the splendid Iberia *of Isaac Albéniz.*

But let us return to the work which you have given us. Since the distant times of Aguado, we lacked a complete Method which would pass on to us the technical progress which Tárrega initiated. You have excellently supplied this want, adding your own magnificent personal contribution, and you have thus benefitted not only the performer but also the composer of keen sensibility, who will find in your Method the stimulus to discover new instrumental possibilities.

Receive my effusive congratulations, then, and the embrace and admiration of your faithful friend.

Manuel de Falla

Granada, December, 1933

TABLE OF CONTENTS

FOURTH COURSE

PREFACE

For reasons beyond our control, this third book of the *Guitar School,* completed in 1936, has not been able to be published until now.

During this lapse of 16 years, its pedagogical contents, applied in private lessons and in the courses under my direction at the National Conservatory of Lisbon have been the most eloquent expression of its effectiveness, in the progress experienced by the students, and in their performances at the end of each course.

However, given the time elapsed, we now believe it appropriate to make a detailed revision of its contents prior to publication.

Perhaps its minute attention to detail seems excessive. Those who do not have at their disposal a good teacher might find it useful. The orderly presentation of the subject matter will allow the rest to adapt it according to their own needs.

The Complementary Studies given at the end of this book[1] are, in recreational form, a compendium of the technical processes subject to both musical and artistic considerations which should be cultivated at the same time.

With the continuous evolution of technique has come pedagogical necessities (not foreseen in earlier Methods), and the logical system to resolve them. Our aim has been to fill in these voids, offering along the way unpublished material that, with assiduity and the necessary time, would yield an effective result in the domain of art.

We do not pretend to exclude with this work that of other authors. No single didactic work can succeed in embracing the subtleties that pedagogy creates in its continuous development. For this reason, we encourage, during certain phases of study, the timely recourse to recommended works by the finest authors.

The basic principles of Tárrega, subjected to all influences, try to develop skills and direct them, in the highest aesthetic sense, towards the continuous development of art, in agreement with the spirit of each age.

EMILIO PUJOL
Professor of guitar at the
National Conservatory of Lisbon
and of vihuela at the Superior
Municipal Conservatory of Barcelona.
September, 1952.

---

1 [Ed. Note: It is our belief that Pujol's original placement of the Complementary Studies at the end of the book resulted in a somewhat disjointed pedagogical continuity. We have therefore relocated the studies and the accompanying texts to their respective positions within the body of this volume, the original paragraph numbers being retained within brackets to indicate their out-of-sequence ordering].

EDITOR'S PREFACE

With this publication in English of Book III of Emilio Pujol's *Escuela Razonada de la Guitarra*, Editions Orphée continues its commitment to a complete translation and re-engraving of the entire Pujol method.

The five volumes that comprise Pujol's *Escuela Razonada* can be likened to a stone being dropped into a still pond. As the concentric circles increase in their circumferences, they clone and amplify the characteristics of the initial stimulus. Thus, as we read with admiration the thorough, thoughtful treatise on instrumental technique which inaugurates the method in Book I, we can appreciate how Pujol's belief that to play the guitar properly, we must first understand it in all its facets, including its history, notation, stringing, and physical characteristics. This same patient exposition is then re-transformed in Book II with an orderly, meticulous presentation of the practical side of guitar technique. Once again Pujol is careful in preparing the student's mind and fingers to be equipped for any musical eventuality that may prey upon a second year guitarist. With the re-publication of Book III, we can again admire the detail with which Pujol approaches his subject. This time, the circle is larger, relying on the same principles of technique but expanding its limits in ever more exhaustive detail. However, where Books I and II are instructive with practical advice on how to hold the hands and move the fingers while working through 98 exercises and 12 studies, Book III seduces the student with a collection of 27 new studies of genuine musical appeal, as well as 147 often inventive and demanding technical exercises of admirable efficacy.

As this edition is a continuation of the Editions Orphée publication of the first two volumes, many of the editorial decisions adopted for those works, and clearly stated in the preface of that publication by its editor, Matanya Ophee, have been followed here. This is based on a desire for a consistent approach to the complete republication of the *Escuela Razonada* as well as a general agreement in editorial methods shared by Mr. Ophee and myself. Rather than repeat that policy here, the reader is encouraged to review its contents both for editorial procedures as well as Mr. Ophee's discussion which places the entire Pujol method in a historical context.

The task of editing this volume has been a two-fold challenge. First, there is the difficulty of faithfully rendering Pujol's formal, somewhat archaic Spanish into a readable English that does not call too much attention to itself as a result of sounding like a translation. For instance, Pujol did not use the terms tirando and apoyando as we currently use them. When he wants an apoyando stroke, he almost invariably describes it as "plucking...[and] resting the finger on the next string." (§ 223) Tirando is referred to as plucking "without resting on the next string." (§ 345) In instances such as these the prevailing and less intrusive terminology (ie., plucking apoyando/plucking tirando) has often been employed.

The second challenge as editor concerns the musical content of this volume which presents a number of decisions. Without question, the most troublesome was Pujol's generous, no, lavish use of fingerings. Were Pujol still alive and I could ask him but one question, it would be why he felt the necessity to supply so much left and right hand fingering with its concomitant array of string and fret indications. Alas, much of it seems dispensable, the context of the exercise or study leaving few alternatives. But to have eliminated much of it, thus liberating Pujol's splendid studies from the plethora of relevant, though often superfluous fingerings which seem to "adorn" every note, would, it seems to me, exceed my authority as editor of Pujol's work. One must hold out the very real possibility that Pujol, ever the devoted Maestro, was teaching his method of good fingering as well as good technique and musicianship. Based on this possible motive, that his fingerings are an integral part of his method, it has been my objective to eliminate only those original fingerings which fall into the most flagrant class of redundancy.

One cannot help feeling, however, that the dark thicket of Arabic numbers, Roman numerals, letters, lines, circled numbers, etc., that all but obliterate the elegant landscapes of musical orthography, do as much harm to the learning curve of the student as they serve as an aid to musical execution. Ophee's remarks describing this as a "pseudo-tablature" (Vol. I, pg. xxi) are an apt characterization. Indeed, Pujol included this same overgrown crop of non-musical symbols in his concert works. While we are grateful for his guidance as to precisely what timbral colors and possible phrasings his fingerings infer, it is the application of fingerings in even the most obvious situations that is disheartening (though even a more modest assortment of fingerings can stifle the interpretive imagination of performers as they tend to co-opt their creativity). Although it is easy to say fingerings can be ignored and our own written in, the geography of the score is as tarnished as an un-zoned country lane with commercial billboards sprouting up like so many eyesores. One can try to overlook them or look around them, but the experience is not the same.

The approach taken in the preparation of this edition has been one of changing as little as possible. In fact, for a work as complex as this, the original contains a striking lack of errors. The most obvious ones have been corrected without comment. Nonetheless, a few deserve mention. Exercises 113, 114, and 115 originally indicated a meter of 6/4. However, they are beamed and sound in 3/2 meter. This has been appropriately corrected.

Other changes, which have been made without comment, are listed below:

Harmonics have been placed in their sounding octave unless otherwise stated.

The C and/or B in advance of a Roman numeral for the barré indication has been eliminated.

The notation of accidentals and key signatures has been modified to reflect current practices.

The notation of the glissando, where the second note is not plucked, has been changed. Pujol's practice was to simply use a diagonal line between the two notes and not indicate a right hand fingering on the second note. The current edition includes a curved slur line above or below the diagonal.

Other editorial changes have been appropriately bracketed as such.

Pujol would be the first to agree that the technique for the guitar is one of constant evolution. The principles as documented here present his view of the "state of the art" as of c.1952. We are now almost 40 years later and it is only natural that we have witnessed further changes to the standard technique of the instrument. However, this should not distract us from a full appreciation of Pujol's Escuela Razonada. For it is in his understanding of the process of learning that we can fully appreciate the timeless wisdom contained herein that has enabled this method to be used worldwide since its initial appearance.

This new edition of Book III of the *Escuela Razonada* has been designed wholly through the use of desktop publishing techniques. This is one of the first examples of a work of music this size to be engraved via music publishing software. The music was engraved with SCORE 3.0 software. The text was written in WordPerfect 5.1. The text font, New Caledonia, was chosen for its similarity to the Scotch typeface employed in Books I and II. Each page of text and musical examples was then assembled through VENTURA 3.0 desktop publishing software. As translator and editor of this project, it has been particularly gratifying to witness the confluence of pedagogical tradition and technological revolution bound together in what I hope will be a significant addition to the literature for the classical guitar.

I wish to express my appreciation to several individuals who helped in preparing this edition. First, admiration and thanks are due Matanya Ophee and Editions Orphée for their persistent dedication toward enriching the literature for the guitar with editions reflecting the rigorous editorial standards which have been characteristic of their publications. I wish to acknowledge the contribution made by Hector Garcia, Emilio Pujol's assistant in Cervera, Spain, for pointing out misprints in the Ricordi edition of this method. Ronald C. Purcell of the University of California at Northridge and Robert Paul Sullivan of the New England Conservatory, Boston, both former students of Maestro Pujol, deserve recognition for their meticulous proof-reading and valuable suggestions, most of which are incorporated in this edition. Finally, I wish to express profound gratitude to my wife, Concha Alborg, whose own erudition and standards of scholarship continue to inspire me.

Peter Segal
Philadelphia,
July, 1991

BOOK III

INTRODUCTION

The road that must be travelled by all who begin the study of any subject, when eagerness is in inverse proportion to their current abilities, is painful and dry. Understanding and persistence are not always enough to master certain difficulties where anxiety or enthusiasm succeed with surprising ease.

For this reason, we strive from the very first to offer even to the most elementary faltering technique, a sense of musicianship which, without clouding the recommended practical ends, should awaken and renew in the spirit of the student the most dynamic and beneficial interests. We believe that, led in this manner along the rugged path towards the mastery of the six rebellious strings of the guitar, the student's fingers will almost imperceptibly dominate the rigors of technique while their musical and artistic sense become developed and affirmed.

Starting then from the basis that the progress of study will be intimately related -- as far as it refers to the movements of the fingers -- with what pertains exclusively to a musical sensibility, we take care to compile in each exercise and study representatives from the different spirits of music (Popular, Classic, Romantic, and Modern) in order to accustom the student to give sway to Music herself, to whom his faculties should humbly serve, while she herself does not deign to serve, as sometimes happens, the capabilities of the artist.

The student, having studied the first and second courses attentively, and having achieved a good realization of the exercises and studies contained therein, shall be in good position to embark without great effort upon the present book in which he will find more difficulties to overcome in order to obtain more positive results.

The technique that is here gradually expounded primarily contains very practical and useful exercises, summarized by a series of complementary "Studies" which require, beyond technical considerations, the care of an essentially musical sensibility. For an effective result, the intense and continued practice of all exercises contained in the present course is indispensable. Toward that same end, whenever the teacher considers it advisable, the complementary Studies can be substituted with works or studies of the great composers. Whosoever intensely desires to master the instrument should realize that the greatest effectiveness lays in the repeated practice of the exercises, above all paying attention to their given instructions. He who uses this book to satisfy more modest aspirations, proceeding carefully through the complementary Studies in their given order, will not waste his efforts needlessly.

He who attains success over the difficulties presented in this volume, will have taken a major step toward the domination of the technique of the guitar and, with well-grounded satisfaction, will find himself in a position to embark upon the performance of important works whose contexts are framed within these given technical parameters.

THIRD COURSE

THEORETICAL-PRACTICAL

LESSON 61

Full Range of the Fingerboard

181. — The notes produced on each string beyond fret XII are the same as those found on the first seven frets of the fingerboard, but raised one octave higher. (See Book I, example 44.)

Example 58   Super-High Region

Commit to memory the notes found on each string beyond fret XII.

LESSON 62

Mobility of the Left Hand

182. — Acknowledging that time is one of the primordial fundamentals of music, one must constantly condense and simplify the movements of the hand and fingers so that all sequences of notes can be produced easily and at the appropriate speed.

To this end, one must be certain that the power and movement of the hand and fingers are applied economically with timely foresight.

183. — Another very essential aspect deserving our attention at the same time as the motion of the fingers of this hand is this: given the fact that the guitar is a *plucked* instrument, the duration of its sound is limited since once a string is plucked, its vibrations tend to diminish in intensity until they fade out entirely; and, if to this condition we add the fact that each stopped note ceases to be heard as soon as the finger leaves the string, we realize how careful the guitarist must constantly be in order to overcome these obstacles and achieve the necessary continuity of sound.

184. — Each finger can adopt a given posture on the string that we may call either *active* or *passive*. It is *active* when the finger *applies pressure* on the string holding it to the fingerboard; and *passive* when, while on a string at a given fret, it maintains its position *without applying pressure*.

Active posture is that which, controlling the string, produces the clarity, duration, and intensity of each note. *Passive* posture permits the effortless shift of position and placement of the fingers and hand without the complete interruption of the vibrations of the string.

The small distance between the plane of the strings and the surface of the fingerboard allows the fingers, which through exercise have developed their natural strength, to be able to maintain contact with those strings against the fingerboard at a given fret with imperceptible effort.

Accordingly, once the duration of a stopped note is complete, the finger that produces it (*active* posture) should release its force, returning the contracted muscles back to their natural flexibility. Thus transformed from *active* to *passive* posture, the finger will then be free to move easily from one string to another, or from one fret to another, near or farther away.

The very flexibility of the *passive* posture is that which gives the necessary agility and precision for the movement of the fingers so they can quickly place themselves in position to play a series of notes without perceptibly stopping the vibrations of each note.

At the beginning, these differences of posture are produced by virtue of the attentive will of the player. With time and practice, they will become intuitive with any finger of the left hand whatsoever.

185. — The left hand moves from left to right and vice versa parallel to the length of the strings, adjusting the flexion of the elbow and wrist such that the arm does not interfere. The forearm, by rotating from the elbow, carries the hand from the lowest to the highest regions of the fingerboard. (See Book I, §209 to §219).[1]

186. — In *ascending* movements (from left to right), the thumb should slide parallel to the other fingers without losing contact with the neck. Upon arriving to play above fret XII, the angle of the wrist will

---

[1] Thus, as the movements of the arm, when directed toward the body, offer more security and stability to the hand than when pushing away from the body, so too are the movements of the fingers toward the palm more secure than when moving in the opposite direction. For this reason, fingers 1 and 2 are preferably used to play two consecutive ascending notes and fingers 4 and 3, the descending ones.

Ascending movements with fingers 1 and 2 correspond, in the direction of the concentric movements of the hand, to the descending movements of fingers 3 and 4. In the same way, ascending movements of fingers 3 and 4 correspond, in the opposite direction of the hand, to the descending movements of fingers 1 and 2.

become more attenuated; the thumb, following the movement of the hand, will slide along the lower edge of the neck taking its position of rest and resistance on the same edge of the fingerboard. (See Book I, fig. 47). This position and the shift of the hand allows each finger to perform freely on all strings, without the hand losing its point of support. (See Book I, § 113).

187. — In *descending* movements (from right to left), the thumb will release its pressure from the neck to place itself at the position of the quadruplet[1] in which the rest of the fingers have to hold the strings. (See Book II, § 115). While the hand moves away from the region above fret XII, the thumb, sliding freely along the back of the neck, will find its normal position.

188. — Shifting the hand from one quadruplet to another, whether near or far, should be done without pushing the hand too far away from the fingerboard and with the fingers positioned in such a way that upon arriving at a new quadruplet, they are able to take their place at the corresponding frets in one single motion. The transverse line of the left hand, which articulates the knuckles at the base of the hand, should maintain with each motion and at whatever place on the fingerboard the same parallel position to the neck and strings.

189. — Reliability of movement principally depends on the flexibility of the muscles that are used. If one wishes to acquire a sure and effortless motion along the fingerboard, one must avoid all stiffness in the fingers, the hand, and the forearm

190. — Fingers 1,2,3, and 4 perform above fret XII just as they do on the rest of the fingerboard, that is, maintaining the angle of their articulations so they can hammer perpendicularly onto the strings.

191. — The left hand shifts along the entire length of the fingerboard by means of one of the following four methods for the movement of the fingers:

1st – By *substitution* of one finger for another, on the same string and at the same fret.

2nd – By *skip* of one or several fingers, to neighboring or distant frets.

3rd – By *glissando* with one or more fingers between consecutive notes.

4th – By crossing fingers over adjacent or non-adjacent frets.

192. — Examples and exercises of the first method:

a) Substitution of finger 2 with finger 1 and vice versa, in two-note sequences.[2]

Example 59

Ascending pattern. Once the G# is plucked, strike the A-natural without the first finger leaving the first fret. Once this note is plucked, run the first finger to the second fret, lifting the second finger at the same time. Repeat this motion for the second, third, and fourth groups of eighth-notes.

Descending pattern. Having struck the second note of the fifth group of eighth-notes (B), run the first finger to the next fret and at the same time position the second finger on the fret previously occupied by the first. Repeat this motion for each successive group of eighth-notes.

---

1 [Ed.: For an explanation of Pujol's use of the terms quadruplet and quintuplet, etc., see Book I, § 101.]

2 The broken line to the right of a number indicates that the finger represented by that number should not lift from the string until the end of the line. The small arrow following a number or broken line indicates the moment when the finger to which it refers, should move. When two or more numbers are encountered vertically, the fingers represented by them should position themselves on the string at the same time stopping the strings in anticipation of the notes to be struck consecutively.

b) *Substitution* of finger 3 with finger 2.

Example 60

The same pattern for fingers 2 and 3 as used in the preceding example for fingers 1 and 2.

c) *Substitution* of finger 4 with finger 3 and vice versa, in two-note sequences.

Example 61

Same remarks for fingers 3 and 4.

d) *Substitution* of fingers 4, 3, and 2 with finger 1 and vice versa, in two-note sequences.

Example 62

Ascending pattern. Having struck the second note of the first group of eighths, run the first finger without leaving the string to the fret which needs to be stopped for the first note of the following group. Repeat the same motion for each successive group of eighths.

Descending pattern. When the first finger positions itself at the fret corresponding to the second note of each group of eighth-notes, the finger corresponding to the first note of the same group will also find its place at the fret which is to be stopped.

e) *Substitution* of finger 2 with finger 1 and vice versa, in three-note sequences.

Example 63

Ascending pattern. Run the first finger to the next fret, once the note held by the third finger is struck, while retaining fingers 1 and 2 on their respective frets as indicated by the broken lines. The same motion will be repeated for the second, third, and fourth groups of eighth-notes.

Descending pattern. Passing from the fifth group of eighths to the sixth and from the sixth to the seventh and then to the eighth group, the first finger moves back one fret each time without leaving the string.

f) *Substitution* of finger 3 with finger 2 and vice versa, in three-note sequences.

Example 64

Ascending pattern. Same arrangement for fingers 2, 3, and 4 as that governing the previous example for fingers 1, 2, and 3.

Descending pattern. Same remarks.

g) *Substitution* of fingers 2 and 3 with finger 1 and of finger 3 with finger 4, in three-note sequences.

Example 65

Ascending pattern. Once the note held by the fourth finger has sounded and having kept fingers 1 and 2 on the string for the first group of eighth-notes, run the first finger to the next fret. Fingers 1 and 3 will move in the same way to go from the third to the fourth group of eighth-notes.

Descending pattern. Moving from the fifth to the sixth group, from there to the seventh, and from the seventh to the eighth, finger 1 will reverse itself one fret at a time without leaving the string. At the same time the fingers that have to stop the rest of the notes of each group will be placed on the corresponding frets.

h) *Substitution* of finger 2 with finger 1 and of finger 3 with finger 4, in four-note sequences.

Example 66

Ascending pattern. Once the note stopped by finger 4 is struck, run finger 1 to the next fret, while retaining fingers 1, 2, and 3 at their respective frets as indicated by the broken lines. The same motion will be repeated for the second and third groups of four eighth-notes.

Descending pattern. Moving from the fourth to the fifth group and from there to the sixth, finger 1 reverses itself one fret each time, simultaneously positioning the other fingers that correspond to the rest of the notes at their respective frets.

i) *Substitution* of finger 4 with finger 1 and vice versa, in four-note sequences.

Example 67

Ascending and descending patterns. Continuing with fingers 2, 3, and 4 in the same manner as the preceding example, finger 1 will proceed to the first note of each group without leaving the string.

193. — Chromatic exercises on each string.

Exercise 99
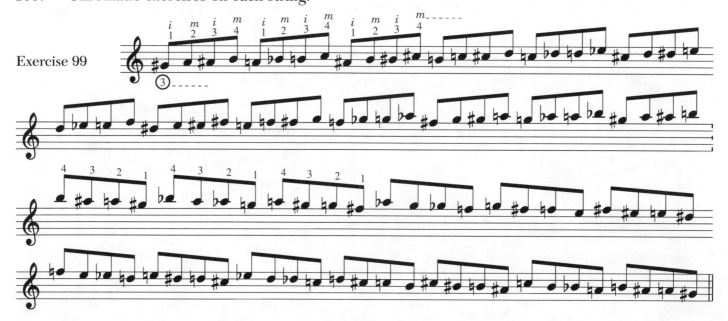

8

Strive for clarity, evenness and fullness of sound and that the action of the left hand in the area above fret XII not obstruct the evenness of the exercise. At first, it will be helpful to play slowly, repeating each group of eighth notes one or more times with the object of affirming the action of the fingers and watching over the movements of the hand.

Likewise, practice with the same relationship of fingers to frets (in the corresponding key) on the fourth, fifth, second, and first strings.

Exercise 100

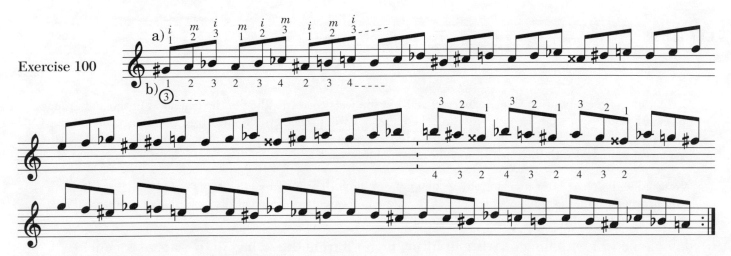

Practice with the two left hand fingerings a) and b) keeping in mind the same remarks expressed in the previous exercise.

Exercise 101

Practice with the three fingerings indicated for the left hand and repeat on the fourth, fifth, second, and first strings.

194. — In general, the exercises fingered with *index* and *middle* for the right hand should likewise be practiced with still more persistence with the *middle* and *annular* fingers because of the weakness of the *annular*. Likewise, the practice of those exercises fingered *middle* and *index* should also be repeated with the fingering *annular* and *middle*.

9

Mobility of the Left Hand

195. — Examples and exercises of the second method.

a) *Skip* of one fret with finger 2 without lifting the first finger from the string, in two-note sequences.

Example 68

Ascending pattern. Position at once fingers 2 and 1 at the frets corresponding to the two notes of the first group of eighth notes. Once the second note is plucked, finger 1 will proceed to the next fret, simultaneously placing the second finger on the fret that corresponds to the first note of the second group. The second, third, and fourth groups are plucked with the repetition of these same movements.

Descending pattern. After plucking the second note of the fifth group of eighth notes held by finger 2, finger 1 will proceed to the fret immediately before. The same movements repeated at the corresponding frets will give the notes of the sixth, seventh, and eighth groups.

b) *Skip* of one fret with finger 3 without lifting finger 2 from the string, in two-note sequences.

Example 69

Ascending and descending pattern. Same arrangement for fingers 3 and 2 as those used in the previous example for fingers 2 and 1.

c) *Skip* of one fret with finger 4 without lifting finger 3 from the string, in two-note sequences.

Example 70

Ascending and descending patterns. Proceed in the same way with fingers 4 and 3.

d) Alternating *skips* of one fret by fingers 2 and 3 respectively, without lifting finger 1 from the string, in two-note sequences.

Example 71

Ascending pattern. Having simultaneously positioned fingers 2 and 1 on the two notes of the first group (A and G#), advance one fret with finger 1 and at the same time, place finger 3 on the first note (B) of the second group. Striking this second note (A), move ahead two frets with finger 1 and place finger 2 on the first note (C) of the third group at the same time. Plucking the B, the fingers will move from the third to the fourth group in the same way they moved from the first to the second.

Descending pattern. After striking the second note of the fifth group of eighths, move back with finger 1 without leaving the string, until the first note of the sixth group at the corresponding fret is plucked. In the same way, proceed successively with the seventh and eighth groups.

e) *Skip* of one fret by fingers 3 and 2 without lifting finger 1 from the string, in three-note sequences.

Example 72

> *Ascending pattern.* Position fingers 3, 2, and 1 at the same time on the three notes of the first group of eighth-notes, lifting successively the first two fingers, and, once the third note is struck, moving finger 1 ahead one fret. Upon arriving at the new fret with this finger, simultaneously position fingers 3 and 2 on the frets that must be stopped for the notes corresponding to the second group. The following two groups require the same movements.

> *Descending pattern.* Moving through the sixth, seventh, and eighth groups, finger 1 moves back each time and fingers 2 and 3 will be positioned successively at the frets that correspond to the second and third notes of each group.

f) *Skip* of one fret by fingers 4 and 3 without lifting finger 2 from the string, in three-note sequences.

Example 73

> *Ascending and descending patterns.* Same scheme for fingers 4, 3, and 2 as used in Example 72 for fingers 3, 2, and 1

g) *Skip* of one fret with fingers 4-3 and 4-2 alternately, without lifting finger 1 from the string, in three note sequences.

Example 74

> *Ascending and descending patterns.* Proceed with fingers 4-2-1 and 4-3-1 according to what corresponds to each group of eighth notes, as in Examples 72 and 73.

h) *Skip* of one fret by fingers 4, 3, and 2 without lifting finger 1 from the string, in four-note sequences.

Ex. 75

Ascending pattern. Having positioned fingers 4, 3, 2, and 1 all in one motion on the four notes of the first group of eighths, lift one at a time off the first three notes and once the fourth is struck, advance finger 1 one fret. This motion should be simultaneous with that of fingers 4, 3, and 2 positioning themselves on the frets that correspond to the first, second, and third notes respectively of the second group. The same movements will be required for the third and fourth groups of eighths.

Descending pattern. Going from the sixth, seventh, and eighth groups, finger 1 moves back one fret and fingers 2, 3, and 4 arrange themselves successively on the frets that correspond to the second, third, and fourth notes of each group.

11

i) *Skip* of several frets by fingers 4, 3, and 2 without lifting finger 1 from the string, in four note-sequences

Example 76

Ascending and descending patterns. Same movements as in Example 75 except that finger 1, when passing from one group to another in the ascending pattern moves the distance necessary to occupy the fret that corresponds to the fourth note of each group, and in the descending pattern will cover the distance which exists between the first notes of each group.

196. — Chromatic exercises on each string.

Exercise 102

Practice with the same fingering and at the same frets on the fourth, fifth, second, and first strings, with right hand fingerings *m-i* and *a-m*.

Exercise 103

Practice with left hand fingerings a) and b) on different strings, and with fingerings *m-i* and *a-m* of the right hand.

Exercise 104

Practice with left hand fingerings a), b), and c) on different strings, and with right hand fingerings *m-i* and *a-m*.

LESSON 64

Mobility of the Left Hand

197. — Examples and exercises of the third method.

a) Ascending *glissando* with the first finger and descending with the third finger.

Example 77

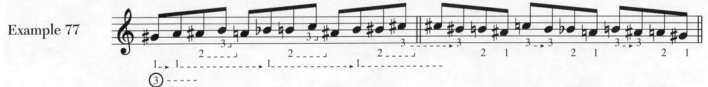

Ascending pattern. After striking the G#, slide the first finger to the next fret. Once the A-natural has sounded and without lifting the first finger, play the two following notes stopping them with fingers 2 and 3 respectively. Having struck the second of these (the last in the group of eighth notes), fingers 2 and 3 are lifted so that the first note of the following group can be sounded. Each ascending group will be the repetition of the same movements in a higher quadruplet.

Descending pattern. Having placed fingers 3, 2, and 1 on frets VI, V, and IV respectively, lift the last two after plucking the first note of the fourth group and move finger 3 to the previous fret, at the same time placing fingers 2 and 1 on frets IV and III. Once the first note of the fifth group is sounded, repeat the same movements with respect to the corresponding frets. The same movements are required for the sixth group.

b) Ascending and descending *glissando* with finger 2.

Example 78

Ascending pattern. After striking the A-natural (the second note of the first group), slide finger 2 to the next fret (A#) in such a way that finger 1 remains prepared on the fret previously occupied by the second. Having struck the B-natural of the same group, fingers 2 and 3 are lifted at the same time and after striking the first note of the second group (A-natural) the same movements will be repeated to produce the notes in the groups that follow.

Descending pattern. After the third group, fingers 3 and 2 remain positioned on frets VI (C#) and V (B#). Having struck the second note of the fourth group (B#), slide finger 2 to its previous fret (B-natural) without abandoning the string while at the same time placing finger 1 on the next fret. Having struck the last note of this group (A#), once again place fingers 3 and 2 on the frets that correspond to the two following notes (C-natural, B) and continue the descending progression in the same way.

c) Ascending and descending *glissando* with the third finger.

Example 79

Ascending and descending patterns. The pattern given in the previous example will govern the groups of these notes substituting fingers 1, 2, and 3 with fingers 2, 3, and 4.

d) Ascending *glissando* with finger 3 and descending with finger 1.

Example 80

Ascending pattern. As indicated by the broken lines, fingers 1 and 2 remain on the string until the moment that finger 3 moves to the next fret.

Descending pattern. Having positioned fingers 3, 2, and 1 on frets VI, V, and IV respectively, finger 1 moves back one fret after striking the B-natural (fret IV). Striking the A#, fingers 3 and 2 position themselves at the same time on the frets that correspond to the first two notes of the fifth group (C-natural and B). These same movements are repeated for the sixth group of eighth notes.

e) Ascending *glissando* with finger 4 and descending with finger 2.

Example 81

Ascending and descending patterns. The same arrangement, applied to fingers 4, 3, and 2.

f) Ascending *glissando* with finger 1 and descending with finger 4.

Example 82

Ascending and descending patterns. The same arrangements govern this example as those for example a), additionally stopping the fifth note of each ascending group and the first in the descending groups with the fourth finger. For the greatest security of movement in the hand, finger 1 will follow the fourth finger with flexibility, and at a natural distance.

g) Ascending *glissando* with finger 2 and descending with finger 3.

Example 83

14

Ascending and descending patterns. Practice as in examples 78 ascending and 79 descending, while also stopping the last note of each ascending group and the first of each descending group with finger 4. Finger 1 should naturally accompany fingers 2 and 3 each time one of them moves to an adjacent fret.

h) Ascending *glissando* with finger 3 and descending *portamento* with finger 2.

Ex. 84

Ascending and descending patterns. Proceed as in examples 79 ascending and 78 descending, while also stopping the fifth note of each ascending group and the first of each descending group with finger 1. Accompany the movements of finger 3 ascending with finger 2 and of finger 2 descending with finger 1.

i) Ascending *glissando* with finger 4 and descending *glissando* with finger 1.

Ex. 85

Ascending pattern. Having struck the fourth note of the first group (B) and keeping each finger in contact with the string (*passive* posture), move the hand to the next quadruplet and strike the fifth note of the group (C). The successive groups are played repeating these same movements.

Descending pattern. After striking the fourth note (B) of the first descending group, the hand moves back one quadruplet sliding finger 1 to the next fret (A#). Having struck this note, fingers 2, 3, and 4 are positioned all at once on the frets where the first three notes of the following group are found (VI, V, and IV); the rest of the groups are successively struck with the same movements.

j) Ascending *glissando* with fingers 1 and 4 and descending *portamento* with fingers 4 and 1.

Ex. 86

Ascending and descending patterns. Fingers 4 and 1 are positioned at the same time to stop the first two notes of the first group. Having struck the G#, continue with the following notes as in examples 82 and 85. — In the fourth group, upon sliding finger 4 to the lower fret, fingers 3, 2, and 1 will simultaneously position themselves on the frets where they have to stop the notes that follow. Having struck the last note of the fourth group, slide finger 1 down one fret and repeat the same movements for the following two groups.

198. — Chromatic exercises on each string.

Exercise 105

Practice with left hand fingerings a), b), c),and d) on different strings and with right hand fingerings *i-m* and *m-a*.

Exercise 106

Practice on different strings, with fingerings *m-i* and *a-m*.

Exercise 107

Practice with left hand fingerings a), b), and c) and right hand formulas *i-m* and *m-a*.

LESSON 65

Mobility of the Left Hand

199. — Examples and exercises of the fourth method.

a) *Crossing* finger 2 with finger 1 and vice versa, on adjacent frets.

Example 87

Ascending pattern. After striking the G#, held by finger 1, position finger 2 on the A-natural. Having struck this second note, finger 2 is lifted and, at the same time, move finger 1 up two frets without applying pressure on the string. The movements should be quick though being sure not to abandon the previous position prematurely.[1]

Descending pattern. Having positioned fingers 2 and 1 at the same time on frets VIII and VII respectively for the fifth group, after striking the D# and D, move the hand back a distance of two frets so the same fingers remain positioned simultaneously on the following two notes, without having lifted the first finger from the string. The same movements are repeated for the following groups. Upon shifting the hand, the fingers should apply the least pressure possible on the string.

b) *Crossing* finger 3 with finger 2 and vice versa, on adjacent frets.

Example 88

Ascending and descending patterns. The same arrangements as those for example 87, applied to fingers 2 and 3.

c) *Crossing* finger 4 with finger 3 and vice versa, on adjacent frets.

Example 89

Ascending and descending patterns. The same arrangements made for examples 87 and 88 applied to fingers 3 and 4.

d) *Crossing* fingers 2, 3, and 4 with finger 1 and vice versa over distant frets.

Example 90

Ascending pattern. Finger 1 remains on G# until the second note has been struck, then slides to the fret which should be stopped for the first note of the second group. The same procedure will be employed in the next group.

Descending pattern. Moving from the fourth to the fifth group, finger 1, without leaving the string, will position itself on the fret belonging to the second note of this group meanwhile striking the first note of this same group. Proceed in the same way to the last group.

---

1 [Ed.: Pujol means that however fast the movement is, each note must be held for its full value.]

e) *Crossing* finger 3 with finger 1, and finger 1 with fingers 2 and 3.

Example 91

Ascending pattern. Fingers 1, 2, and 3 will remain positioned on their respective frets while the three notes of the first group are struck. Successively lifting fingers 2 and 3, move finger 1 up three frets to strike the first note of the second group. The same movements are repeated for each successive group.

Descending pattern. Having positioned fingers 3, 2, and 1 on frets IX, VIII, and VII respectively for the first descending group, lift the first two fingers successively. Once the final note of the fourth group is struck, slide finger 1 down three frets, simultaneously positioning fingers 3 and 2 at the frets which correspond to the first and second notes of the next group.

f) *Crossing* fingers 3 and 4 with finger 2 and vice versa, on adjacent frets.

Example 92

Ascending and descending patterns. The same disposition as that for example 91 applied to fingers 2, 3, and 4.

g) *Crossing* fingers 2-4 and 3-4 with finger 1, and of fingers 3-1 and 2-1 with finger 4, on non-adjacent frets.

Example 93

Ascending and descending patterns. Alternating the succession of fingers 2 and 4 with that of fingers 3 and 4, finger 1 will proceed as in example 90. Moving from the third to the fourth group, finger 4 will slide on the string until arriving at the fret that corresponds to the first note of this group.

h) *Crossing* fingers 2, 3, and 4 with finger 1 and vice versa.

Example 94

Ascending and descending patterns. The directions given in example 91 for fingers 1, 2, and 3 likewise govern this example, applied to fingers 1, 2, 3, and 4. Finger 1 does not lift from the string during the progression of ascending or descending groups.

i) *Crossing* of different fingers to distant frets.

Example 95

18

Ascending and descending patterns. Proceed as in example 93 applying the same instructions to fingers 1, 2, 3, and 4, always moving finger 1 to the first fret of each quadruplet where the four notes of each group are formed, in the ascending patterns as well as the descending ones.

200. — Chromatic exercises on each string.

Exercise 108

Practice with fingerings *i-m*, *m-i*, *m-a*, and *a-m* on different strings, seeing that the movements of the hand, when moving between quadruplets, are made in a precise and natural way.

Exercise 109

Practice on different strings with right hand fingerings *i-m* and *m-a*, accentuating the first note of each group of eighth-notes.

Exercise 110

Practice in the same manner as the previous exercise, with right hand fingerings *m-i* and *a-m*.

201. — To combat the difficulty presented by crossing the fourth finger with the first in ascending movements and the reverse crossing in the descending movements, it will be helpful to concentrate on these difficulties separately by means of the following formulas.

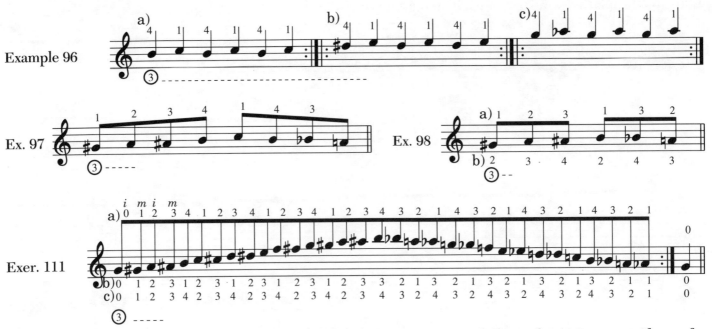

Practice with fingerings a), b), and c) for the left hand, repeating with formulas *m-i*, *m-a*, and *a-m* for the right hand.

202. — Memorize and practice Complementary Study XIII.

General Instructions for the Complementary Studies

[330.] — The purpose of the present Studies in which certain aspects of guitar technique are summarized is not only to surmount in each one the difficulties that they present by themselves, but to affirm at the same time with practice and mastery, an instrumental, musical, and aesthetic feeling that orients and awakens in the student, the abilities of the interpreter which must guide the performance of one's repertoire.

[331.] — To bring this about effectively, it is necessary that they are read paying close attention to the exact value of each note, without altering the indicated fingerings, and committing each Study to memory (see Book I, §§225, 226), until, being able to perform them at the indicated tempo and with the given nuances, one succeeds in infusing them with the spirit of the soul that only its own depth and sensitivity permits.

[332.] — He who begins patiently from the first exercise seeking perfection as Tárrega would wish, will be successful rather than the impatient one who stumbles over difficulties without correcting them hoping too late to submit to the discipline that true art demands. It is more difficult to correct an acquired bad habit than to try to avoid it from the beginning. The sum of values in the artist's work not only resists the corrosive action of time and criticism, but, on reaffirming one's own confidence, elevates the kind of art to which it applies and acquires the persuasive admiration of those who appreciate it.

Specific Instructions for Study XIII

[333.] — Alternation of fingers *i-m*, in chromatic succession on different strings and in different areas of the fingerboard.

a) Strict alternation of fingers *i-m*.

20

b) Displacement of the left hand should not cause discontinuity in the melodic line.

c) Suggest the rhythmic accent in measures 27, 28, and 29.

d) Gracefulness requires the use of the glissando when going from measure 30 to 31.

e) Study slowly and once mastered, gradually repeat the movements at faster and faster tempos until the indicated velocity is achieved or surpassed while observing the given nuances.

Study XIII

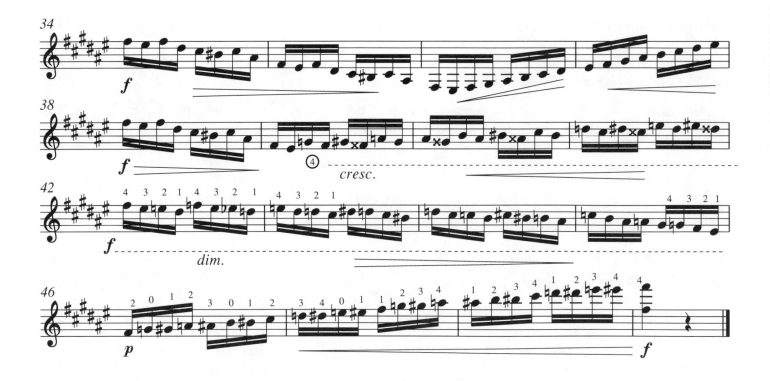

LESSON 66

Extension[1] of the Hand

203. — The possibility of separating the fingers from themselves permits the hand to encompass a distance greater than a quadruplet without the necessity of displacing itself.

204. — Because the motion of opening the fingers is opposite to concentric movement (more natural to the hand) it is necessary to achieve facility of motion through exercises which, developing the strength and elasticity of the fingers, will avoid contractions and sharp movements that tend to de-sensitize and immobilize the hand.

Regardless of how open the fingers are, *the hand should never change its perpendicular position to the neck.* It is necessary, as well, that the fingers, as they apply pressure to the strings, concentrate their force in the fingertip.

205. — Frequent repetition in each exercise develops flexibility and power of certain flexor muscles in the hand and fingers, permitting them to realize passages that at first were difficult, if not impossible.

206. — The quickest to develop is the stretch between fingers 1 and 2. — More difficult is the stretch of finger 4 and more still is that of finger 3 in that it is anatomically less favorable to independence.

Exercise 112

Repeat each measure several times, likewise practicing at quadruplets VIII, VII, VI, and V.

---

1 [Ed.: i.e., reach.]

The stretching of finger 4 toward the fret contiguous to that which would naturally correspond to it, must be achieved without altering the flexibility of the hand or that of the other fingers. In spreading finger 4, do so in such a way that finger 2 does not move on the fret which it occupies, and that this anchoring does not cause the hand or the fingers to contract.

Exercise 113

Practice slowly with the same arrangement of fingers and frets on all strings with right hand fingerings *m-i* and *a-m*, while maintaining flexibility in the hand and fingers, and with the greatest possible clarity for each note.

Exercise 114

Also exercise with the same arrangement of frets and fingers on different strings, with right hand fingerings *i-m* and *m-a*.

Exercise 115

Likewise practice on several strings with right hand fingerings *i-m* and *m-a*.

Exercise 116

Practice likewise on the fifth, third, second, and first strings with the same arrangement of frets and fingers and with right hand fingerings *i-m* and *m-a*.

Exercise 117

Repeat on other strings with right hand fingerings *m-i* and *a-m*.

Exercise 118

Practice in the same way as the previous exercises with right hand fingerings *i-m* and *m-a*.

Exercise 119

Repeat on different strings as before, with right hand fingerings *m-i* and *a-m*.

LESSON 67

Complement to the Previous Lesson

207. — Diatonic exercises on each string.

Exercise 120

Practice the same way as the exercises in the previous lesson, shifted to different strings and keeping the same arrangement of frets and fingers.

Exercise 121

Practice as in Exercise 120, on different strings with right hand fingerings *i-m*, *m-i*, *m-a*, and *a-m*.

Exercise 122

Likewise, practice on different strings with the right hand fingerings used for the two previous exercises.

Exercise 123

Repeat the same format as the preceding exercises.

208. — Major and minor scales on each string.

Exercise 124

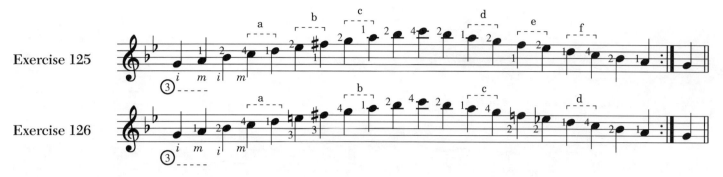

Exercise 125

Exercise 126

Practice, transposing to each string with the four right hand fingerings *i-m, m-i, m-a,* and *a-m.* Give extra attention to the shift from one position to the next (letters a, b, c, d, e, f), to better assure the equality and evenness between these notes.

209. — Work on Study XIV.

Specific Instructions for Study XIV

[334.] — Same practice for the right hand on different strings, in diatonic succession.

a) Be certain to use the indicated right hand fingering.

b) Avoid discontinuity in the melodic line in measures 13 to 16 and 31 to 33.

c) Work in the same progressive order as the previous Study.

Study XIV

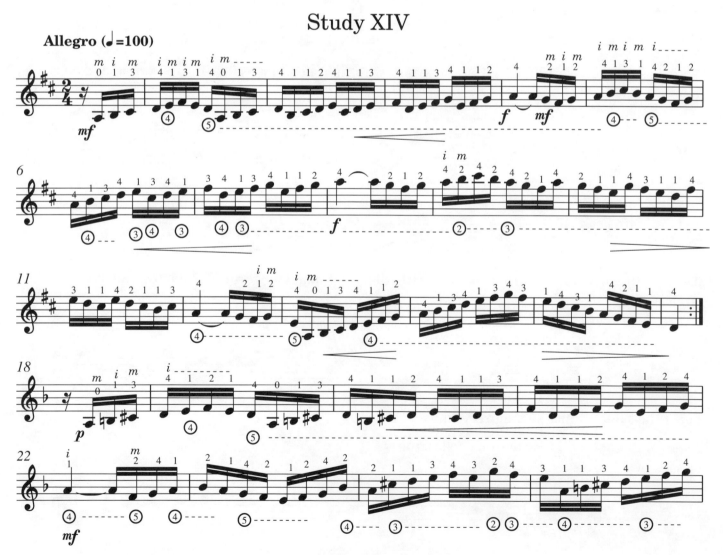

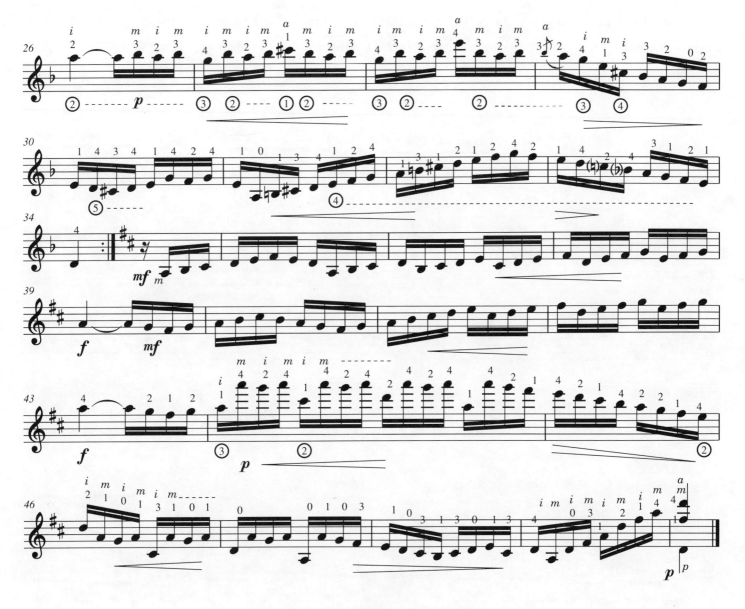

LESSON 68

Mobility of the Left Hand Combined with Simultaneous Movement of the Fingers

210. — Chromatic and diatonic thirds on adjacent strings.

Exercise 127

Simultaneously position the fingers that form the interval of a third being careful that the crossing of fingers ($\frac{3}{4}$) by fingers ($\frac{1}{2}$) and vice versa, are effortless and precise movements. Practice with right hand fingerings *m-a* and *i-m* equally.

Exercise 128

Position the fingers that form the interval of a third all at the same time, paying attention to the movements of the left hand as in the previous exercise. Likewise practice with the right hand *a-m*.

Exercise 129

Accent the first note of each triplet and also practice with the right hand fingering *m-a*.

Exercise 130

Finger 3 should not leave the string from the second group of eighth notes to the next to last group. Repeat with fingering *m-a*.

Keep finger 1 on the third string for the entire exercise. Practice with the same arrangement of frets and fingers on the fourth and fifth strings ($\frac{4}{5}$) and the first and second ($\frac{1}{2}$).

Exercise 131

Since it is also possible to finger this succession of thirds with fingers 2, 3, and 4 in place of 1, 2, and 3, it will be beneficial to alternate practice between the two fingerings.

Also alternate with right hand fingerings *m-i* and *a-m*.

211. — Work on Study XV.

Specific Instructions for Study XV

[335.] — Alternation of the same fingers on adjacent or non-adjacent strings.

a) The intervals of successive thirds (major and minor) on neighboring strings should be formed at the same time by the corresponding left hand fingers.

b) Take special care to avoid unwanted glissandi[1] (or glissandi not indicated) that are always produced when the finger corresponding to the second and fourth sixteenth-notes of each group (lower string of the thirds), while passing to another fret, does not lessen its pressure on the string. This observation does not hold, naturally, for the glissandi expressly marked in measures 27 and 30.

c) Since the eighth-notes are the ones that carry the principal melody on the upper string of the two which the fingers play, this string should be made to stand out by finger *m* and seconded by the index, *i*, on the lower string, according to the marked dynamics and the feeling in which it should be performed.

Study XV

---

1 Unintentional glissando which anticipates the sound of a note and which is produced by the displacement of the fingers along the same string.

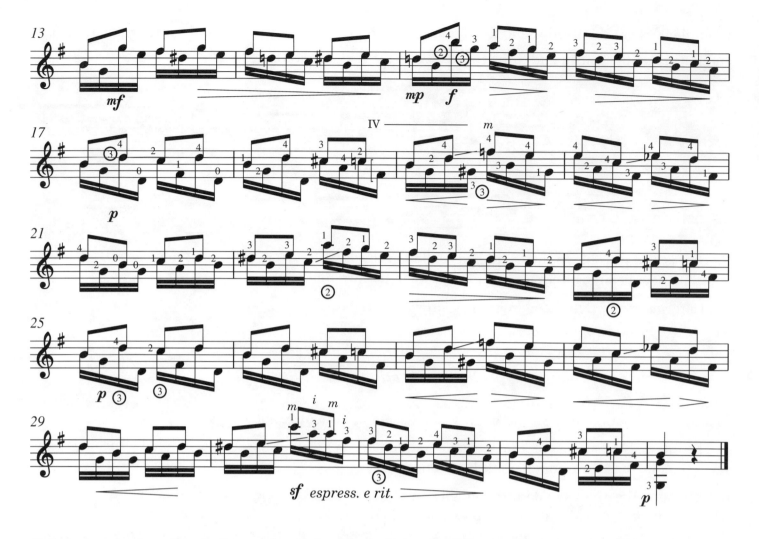

d) Practice slowly at first before giving it the required tempo and expression.

LESSON 69

Use of the Barré While Increasing the Distance Between the Fingers

212. — Chromatic and diatonic scales on all strings within the range of a quintuplet.

Exercise 132

The first finger should remain extended across the six strings at the fifth fret. This finger has the tendency to move toward the next higher fret as the other fingers spread more and more. So that this exercise is beneficial, one should make a special effort to sustain the barré securely at its position while the other fingers play on the second and first strings.

Exercise 133

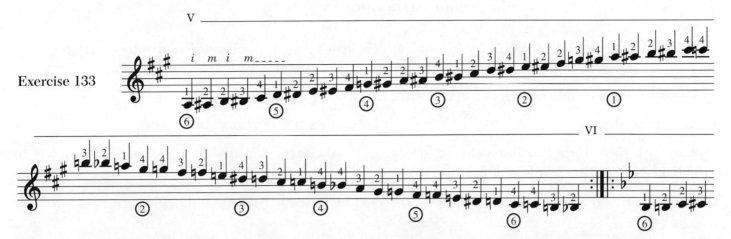

Practice slowly at quintuplets VI, VII, VIII, and IX. In that the assiduous practice of this exercise develops the strength of the barré, it should also be practiced at quintuplets I to IV.

213. — We recommend the daily practice of this very beneficial exercise until the pupil is able to repeat it at each quintuplet without getting tired, from fret I to IX and back again to I, playing it slowly and without interruption. Practice with the four right hand fingerings *i-m*, *m-i*, *m-a*, and *a-m*.

Exercise 134

Exercise 135

Exercise 136

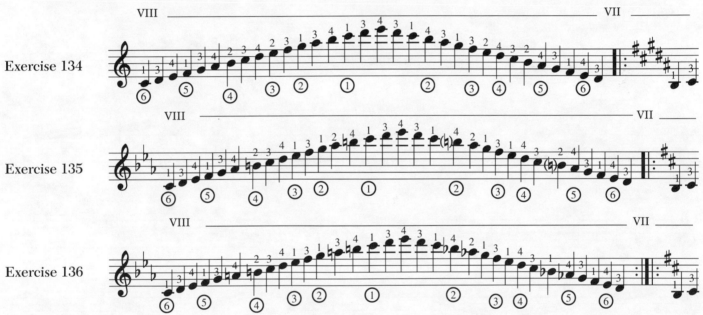

Repeat each exercise beginning at quintuplet VIII, progressively descending to quintuplet I if the strength of the barré permits.

Exercise 137

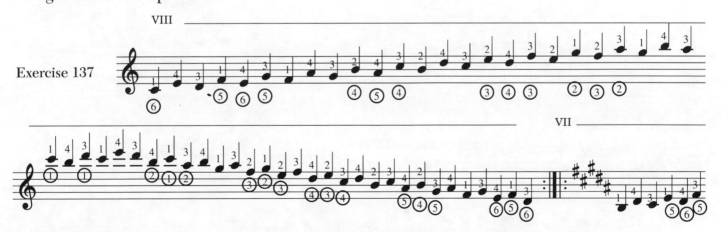

Practice in the same way as exercise 133 with all four right hand fingerings.

214. — Work on Study XVI.

[336.] — Strength of the Barré. Major and minor scales moving perpendicularly to the strings, for fingers *i-m* and *m-a*, within the range of a quintuplet.

a) Strive for clarity and evenness of sound without allowing the barré to yield its position.

b) An accent should be lightly placed on the first note of each group of sixteenth-notes.

c) Although this Study calls for velocity for its auditory effect, it is advisable to practice it slowly to effectively add to the development of the strength of the *barré*.

d) Concentrate on measures 19 to 24 and 43 to 48 to obtain security and avoid haphazard interruptions.

Study XVI

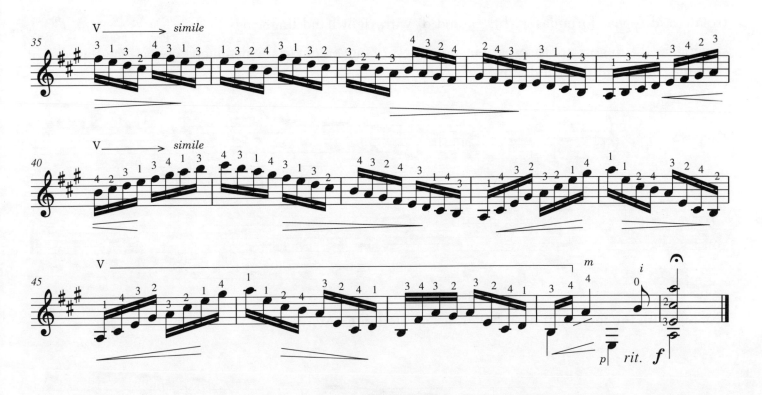

LESSON 70

Simultaneous Action of the Thumb with the Other Fingers

215. — Chromatic scales on each string with different distances for the thumb.

Exer. 138

Isolate and repeat formulas a), b), c), and d) with right hand fingerings $(\frac{i-m}{p})$, $(\frac{m-i}{p})$, $(\frac{m-a}{p})$, *and* $(\frac{m-a}{p})$, striving for the fingers not to lose their suppleness of movement as the distance between the thumb and the other fingers of this hand grows.

Exercise 139

Practice with the four right hand fingerings applied in Exercise 138.

Exercise 140

Practice with the same right hand fingerings.

Exercise 141

Exercise 142

Apply the same right hand fingerings to these exercises striving to attain as much evenness as possible in the scales without making mistakes on those notes played by the *thumb*.

216. — Work on Study XVII.

Specific Instructions for Study XVII

[337.] — Agility of both hands. Scales both parallel and perpendicular to the strings while simultaneously using the thumb.

a) Observe the fingerings corresponding to each hand.

b) Heed the rhythmic value and intensity of the melodic line according to the indicated dynamics lightly accenting the first note of each triplet, especially those of a rhythmic character.

c) Bring out the expressiveness of the melody in measures 19, 20, and 21.

d) Work slowly to play it better at the given tempo.

e) For the required agile, graceful, and expressive result, it is necessary to use as much suppleness in the hands and flexibility in the fingers as possible.

If well studied, it is not only beneficial but also a great showpiece.

Study XVII

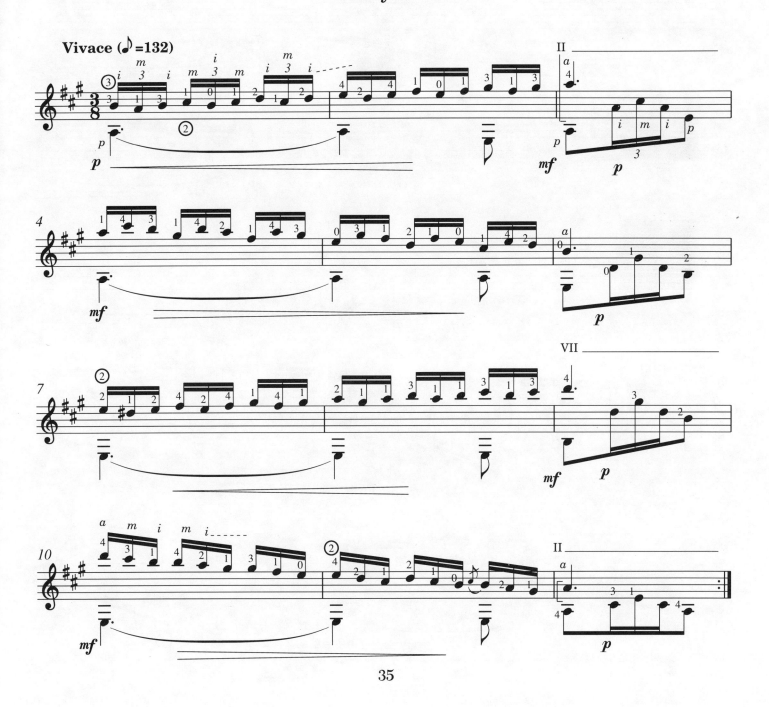

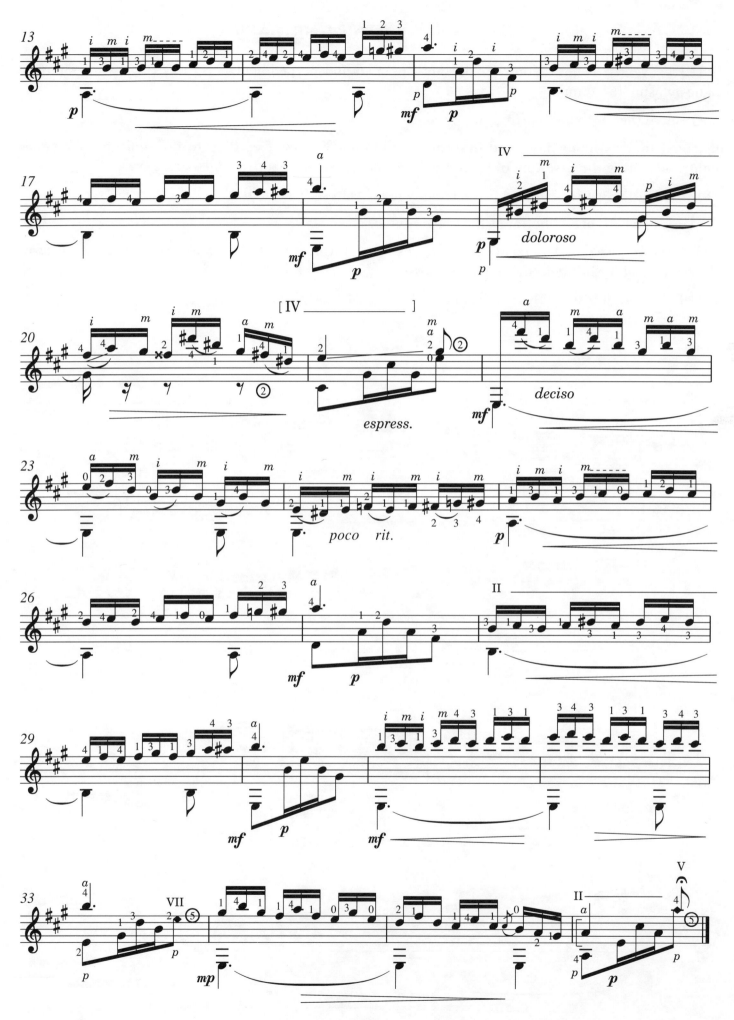

Increasing the Mobility of the Thumb

217. — Chromatic scales while simultaneously plucking with the thumb on each note.

Exercise 143

Same arrangement as for Exercise 138. Practice according to formulas a,) b), c) and d) with the four different right hand fingerings. Compelling the *thumb* to pluck more frequently, its movements ought to be smaller without allowing the concentration of power in its tip joint. Avoid leaps and hazardous contractions of the hand.

Exercise 144

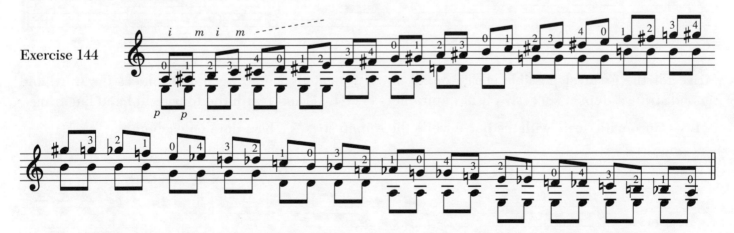

Same arrangements as for Exercise 140. Practice with the four right hand fingerings simultaneously with the *thumb*.

218. — Chromatic scale with the *thumb* while simultaneously plucking every note with another finger.

Exercise 145

Try not to obstruct the sound of the notes when the *thumb* and *another finger* simultaneously pluck on adjacent strings. Practice with the four usual fingerings.

219. — Diatonic scale with the *thumb* while plucking with the fingers on every other note.

Exercise 146

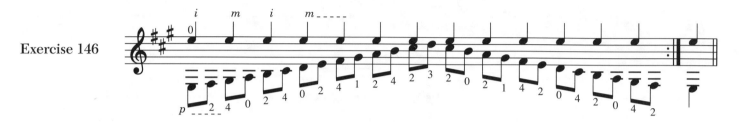

Practice with the same right hand fingerings indicated for the previous exercises.

LESSON 72

Simultaneous Notes Sustained by the Barré

220. — Chromatic scale with the barré while striking the bass with the *thumb* on alternate notes.

Exercise 147

Strive for the greatest possible clarity on all notes, especially when the thumb plucks the third and second strings. Repeat successively at quintuplets IV, III, II, and I with the four right hand fingerings.

221. — Chromatic scale with the barré while the *thumb* strikes a bass note on each note.

Exercise 148

Same observations as those for exercise 147.

222. — Scale in sixths with the barré; more independence of the *thumb*.

Exercise 149

Practice at different quintuplets with fingerings $(\frac{m}{p} - \frac{a}{p})$ and $(\frac{i}{p} - \frac{m}{p})$.

223. — Work on Study XVIII.

Specific Instructions for Study XVIII

[338.] — Using the thumb simultaneously with the index, middle, and annular fingers. a) Strive to keep the notes struck by the thumb in equal proportion relative to the intensity of the notes struck by the other fingers, so that they do not overpower the principal melodic line. b) Be careful to give each voice the expressive feeling proper to its phrasing and in agreement with the indicated dynamics. c) Observe the exact value of the syncopated notes in measures 23, 26, and 28. d) Measures 30 and 31 require special attention.

Study XVIII

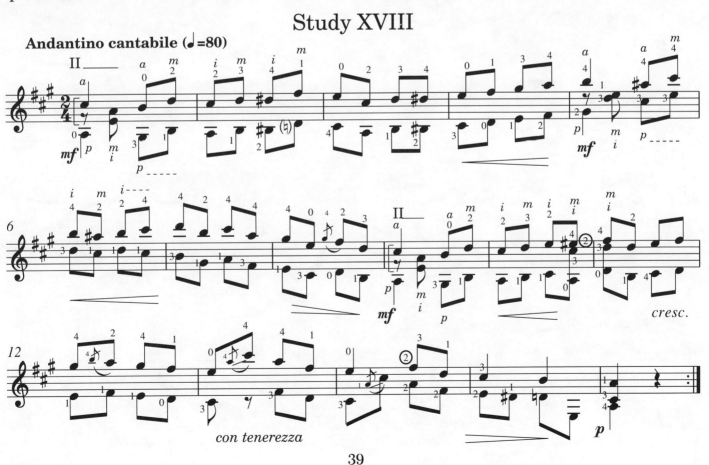

LESSON 73

Three-note Arpeggios. Index, Middle, and Annular Fingers on the Same String

224. — Practice the following left hand formula, striking each note six times with right hand fingerings a) and repeat successively with formulas[1] b), c), d), e), and f), plucking apoyando on each note. Strive to obtain the greatest equality and evenness possible between the notes, maintaining the balance of the right hand, without changing the order of the fingers in any of the formulas for this hand.

Exercise 150

Since these mechanisms can be applied to each string in the respective key of the open note, it will be useful to practice them on each string while changing the formula. When practicing on the sixth string, attempt to overcome the need of a resting point due to the lack of a lower string so that it should not impede the security of plucking nor the balance of the hand.

225. — Work on Study XIX.

Specific Instructions for Study XIX

[339.] — Consecutive movement of the index, middle, and annular fingers on the same string.

a) Accent those notes marked with the sign > .

b) Observe the left hand fingering, given frets and strings to produce the notes without change.

c) At first, work slowly; repeat with right hand formula *a-m-i*.

d) Gradually accelerate the tempo in agreement with the given dynamics until achieving the velocity and continuity required by its particular character.

Study XIX

43

LESSON 74

Three-note Arpeggio on Two Adjacent Strings
Moving the Annular Finger To the Upper String

226. — Proceed as in the preceding lesson, observing the firmness of the stroke, the equality between the notes, and the flexibility and discipline of the fingers.

Exercise 151

Exercises 127, 130, and 131 will offer the pupil different left hand formulas which can likewise be applied to the arpeggios of the present exercise.

LESSON 75

Three-note Arpeggio on Two Adjacent Strings
Moving the Middle and Annular Fingers to the Upper String

227. — Proceed as in the previous lesson observing the same directions.

Exercise 152

To achieve equalization in striking the strings, it will be useful to practice these arpeggios not only on other strings, but varying the point of attack between the bridge and the sound-hole.

LESSON 76

Three-note Arpeggios on Three Adjacent Strings. One Finger for Each String

228. — Since this exercise is the continuation of the previous exercises, it will be practiced according to the same instructions.

Exercise 153

The pupil will find more variety in this exercise practicing the same mechanisms on the first, second, and third strings. In this case, starting with the key of C major, ascending by diatonic thirds on the first and second strings until arriving at the octave of the key, and gradually descending, taking care that during the entire exercise the G of the open third string is maintained as a pedal note.

LESSON 77

Three-note Arpeggio on Two Non-adjacent Strings and Another One Adjacent. Separation Between Middle and Index Fingers

229. — Proceed as in the previous exercises, being careful that the necessity of striking with the first finger on a non-adjacent string does not cause the other fingers to open in the form of a fan nor straighten out. These difficulties could alter the necessary flexibility in the fingers and stability in their plucking motion.

Exercise 154

One should be able to achieve variety in this exercise practicing the same right hand mechanisms or formulas on the first, second and fourth strings. In which case, starting with the key of G major, one will ascend by diatonic thirds on the higher strings until arriving at the octave and gradually descending, taking care that during the entire exercise, the D of the open fourth string acts as a pedal.

LESSON 78

Three-note Arpeggio on Two Adjacent Strings and Another One Non-adjacent. Separation Between Middle and Annular Fingers

230. — Proceed as in the previous exercises seeing that the separation of the distance of attack between the middle and annular fingers does not compromise the hand.

Exercise 155

a) i ma i ma b) i a m i a m c) a i m a i m d) a m i a m i e) m a i m a i f) m i a m i a

To vary the left hand formula, simply transpose to the fourth, third, and first strings with the same arrangement of frets and fingers. (Transpose a fourth above; key of E major.)

LESSON 79

Three-note Arpeggio on Three Non-adjacent Strings.
Separation Between Index-Middle and Middle-Annular Fingers

231. — Since this exercise complements the two preceding, the same instructions should be followed.

Exercise 156

a) i ma i ma b) i a m i a m c) a i m a i m d) a mi a m i e) m a i ma i f) m i a m i a

The left hand formula will be varied, transposed with the same arrangement of frets and fingers to the sixth, fourth, and second strings (key of B Major).

232. — Work on Study XX.

Specific Instructions for Study XX

[340.] — Consecutive movement of the index, middle, and annular fingers on different strings.

a) Follow the indicated fingerings for both hands.

b) Sustain the notes for their entire duration, avoiding discontinuity of sound when shifting the left hand from one position to another.

c) Project the melody linking the phrases together.

d) The G# of measure 25 requires strength in the barré.

e) Shape the entire Study according to what is indicated, expressing it with the sensitivity it requires.

Study XX

Apoyando and Tirando[1] *Combined*

233. — Apply the following left hand formula to right hand mechanisms a), b), c), and d).

Exercise 157

Practice the triplets apoyando and the chord following, tirando. Try to achieve the maximum equality and evenness possible between the notes.

It is possible to vary the left hand formula applying the same arrangement of frets and fingers on the fourth and third strings ($\frac{3}{4}$), fifth and fourth ($\frac{4}{5}$), and sixth and fifth ($\frac{5}{6}$) since each pair is tuned to the same interval.

234. — Work on Study XXI.

Specific Instructions for Study XXI

[341.] — Two-note chords alternating with successive movement of the index, middle, and annular fingers.

a) Follow the fingerings for both hands.

b) Accent the first note of each triplet and the chords marked with the > sign .

c) The chords marked with an asterisk should have a little vibrato to give them greater expressive inflection.

d) This Study requires a joyful and spirited air.

e) The notes following the chord of the third measure from the end should be attacked with decisiveness and a feeling of precise affirmation.

---

1 [Ed.: Pujol does not use the term "tirando" choosing instead "sin apoyo," ie., without support.]

Study XXI

LESSON 81

Three-note Arpeggio Plucking Simultaneously with the Thumb on the First Note

235. — Practice in successive quadruplets according to the following formulas, using apoyando except when the index or annular finger coincides with the thumb on an adjacent string.

Exercise 158

236. — Work on Study XXII.

Specific Instructions for Study XXII

[342.] — Consecutive movement of the index, middle, and annular fingers on two strings while plucking simultaneously with the index finger and thumb.

a) Pay attention to the fingerings of both hands.

b) Avoid unwanted glissandi on the successive thirds when they occur between two notes of the arpeggio on adjacent strings. At the same time, be careful that the notes played simultaneously with the thumb are clear and that those played with the middle finger do not interrupt the sound of those played on the next string with the index finger.

Dynamic and tempo markings are not present in the manuscript we believe to be a copy of the original. We indicate them according to our recollection of the interpretation given by the author[1] himself.

---

1 [Ed.: i.e., Tárrega.]

Study XXII
(Tárrega)

Allegretto (♩.=120)

FOURTH COURSE

LESSON 82

Four-Note Arpeggio Played with Index, Middle and Annular Fingers. Arpeggio on one String

237. — Since these arpeggios complement the three-note arpeggios that the pupil has already practiced in lessons 73, 74, 75, 76, 77, 78, and 79, the same instructions that were given for them will be applied to these exercises.

Apply right hand mechanisms a), b), c), d), e), f), g), h), i), j), k), and l) to the following left hand formula, resting each stroke on the next string. Likewise, strive for equality of sound, protecting the balance of the hand and the flexibility of the fingers without altering the fingering in the repetition of each mechanism.

Exercise 159

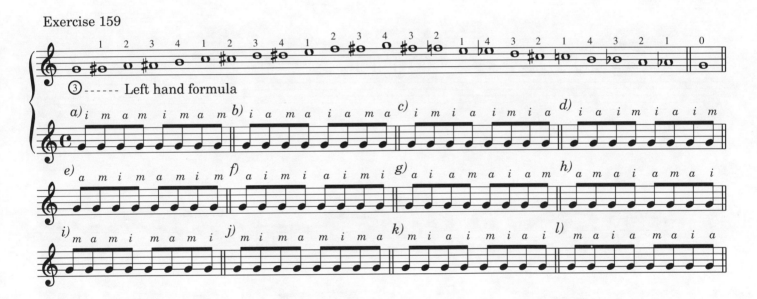

The instructions for Exercise 150 can be applied to these mechanisms. (Lesson 73).

238. — Work on Study XXIII.

Specific Instructions for Study XXIII

[343.] — Use of right hand formula *i-m-a-m* and its inversion *a-m-i-m*, on the same string while simultaneously using the thumb on the first note.

a) Tune the sixth string an octave lower than the open fourth string.

b) Pay attention to the evenness and equality of intensity of the sixteenth notes as well as the melodic continuity and changes of tempo.

c) The *cadenza* that follows measure 20 should begin slowly and accelerate a little in the sextuplets. A little more intensity of sound and expressive power in the notes should be given in the *lento* that finishes the *cadenza*.

Apart from its didactic aim, this Study evokes the suggestion of a distant landscape with the bluish *chiaroscuro* of a fall moon amidst rustling leaves.

Study XXIII

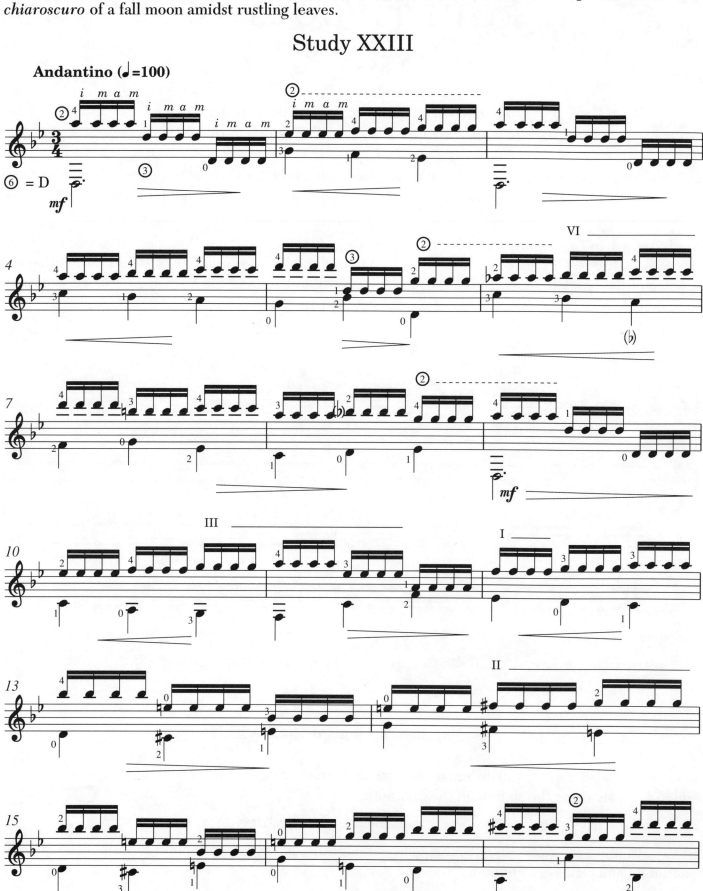

55

Four-Note Arpeggio on Two Adjacent Strings.
Movement of the Annular Finger to the Upper String

239. — Proceed as in Exercise 151 of Lesson 74.

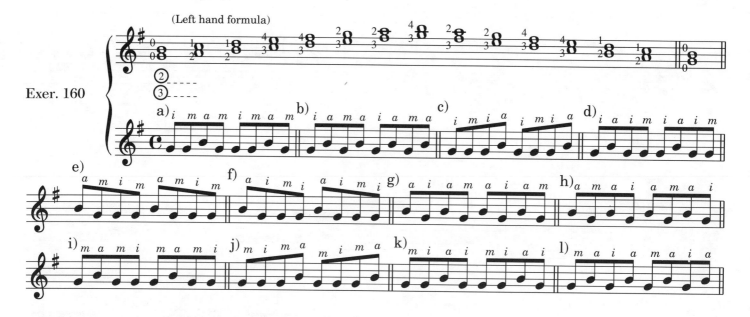

The pupil, already familiar with the left hand formulas cited in Lesson 75, can make use of them to give variety to these mechanisms.

240. — Work on Study XXIV.

Specific Instructions for Study XXIV

[344.] — Use of the formula *a-m-i-m* on two strings emphasizing the *annular* finger.

a) Bring out the melody found on the third string with the *annular* finger while the *middle* and *index* fingers sustain both the even tempo and intensity of the pedal note on the open fourth string.

b) All fingers should be played *apoyando*.

c) Independent of the evenness of the notes played on the fourth string by the middle and index fingers, one should be sensitive to the appropriate expression of the melody struck by the *annular* finger on the third string.

d) Work slowly at first, repeating successively with growing velocity always such that the clarity and evenness of the notes and flexibility of the hands are not compromised.

e) The *D* of the open 4th string, struck successively by the *index* and *middle* fingers should produce the effect of the same note continued by repetition.

Study XXIV
(on two strings)

(Melody on third string throughout study.)

LESSON 84

Four-note Arpeggio on Two Adjacent Strings.
Transition of the Middle and Annular Fingers to the Upper String

241. — Apply the following mechanisms a), b), c), d), e), f), g), h), i), j) k), and l) to this left hand formula.

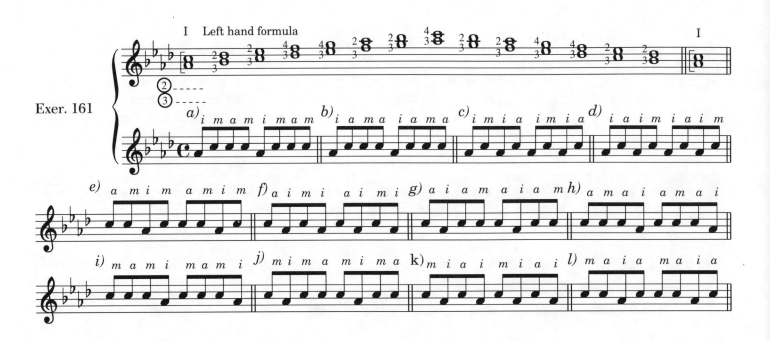

The same instructions for Lesson 75 apply to this exercise.

242. — Work on Study XXV.

[345.] — Use of the formula *i-m-a-m* playing simultaneously with the *thumb* and *index* fingers.

a) Enclosing the 24 measures of this Study are a prelude and postlude of eight and nine measures respectively which should be played *apoyando* and the rest, [ie. mm 9 - 32] *tirando*.[1]

b) Be careful with the action of *i-p* on the same string when moving from measure 1 to 2 and from 2 to 3, as well as 33 to 34 and from there to 35.

c) From measure 9 to 32, the notes corresponding to fingers *m-a-m* should be produced with the greatest possible clarity, equality, and evenness.

d) The notes played by the *index* finger should not be cut short by the *middle* finger on the next string touching them.

e) One can also practice the middle section from measures 9 to 32 *as an apoyando exercise* in which case overruling the previous stipulation, d).

f) Bear in mind the fingerings of both hands as well as the dynamic and tempo changes.

Study XXV is found on page 60.

LESSON 85

Four-note Arpeggio on Three Adjacent Strings. One Finger for Each String

243. — Apply the following right hand mechanisms to this left hand formula :

Exer. 162

For this exercise, use the instructions referred to for Exercise 153, given in Lesson 76.

---

1 [Ed.: The teacher may wish to alter Pujol's instructions which generally stress the use of the apoyando stroke; the current practice in guitar technique seems to emphasize it less.]

Study XXV

LESSON 86

Four-note Arpeggio on Three Adjacent Strings.
Repetition of Each Finger on the Same String

244. — Apply the right hand mechanisms that accompany the following left hand formula, exacting as in Exercise 153 of Lesson 76, equality and evenness in the notes, firmness in striking the strings, and flexibility and precision in the movement of the fingers.

245. — Work on Study XXVI.

Specific Instructions for Study XXVI

[346.] — Alternating arpeggios and scales.

a) The performance of this Study requires agility in both hands, security in the changes in the left hand and resolute striking of the strings.

b) Bring out the notes of the arpeggios that are struck by the *annular* finger, those notes in the scale passages, and those in bars 7, 16, and 25 as their melodic sense requires.

c) The true effect of this Study will not be attained if one does not play it with the liveliness accorded its given tempo, as well as the rhythmic accent and dynamics indicated for its interpretation.

For the purpose of correct page turns, this page left intentionally blank

Study XXVI

65

LESSON 87

Four-Note Arpeggio on Two Non-Adjacent Strings and One Adjacent One.
Separation Between the Middle and Annular Fingers

246. — Apply the following right hand mechanisms to the present left hand formula, developing the separation between the index and middle fingers, without hindering the firmness in striking the strings, the flexibility of the fingers, and the equality between the notes.

Exer. 164

LESSON 88

Four-Note Arpeggio on Two Adjacent Strings and One Non-Adjacent.
Separation Between Middle and Annular Fingers

247. — Apply the right hand mechanisms that accompany the following left hand formula.

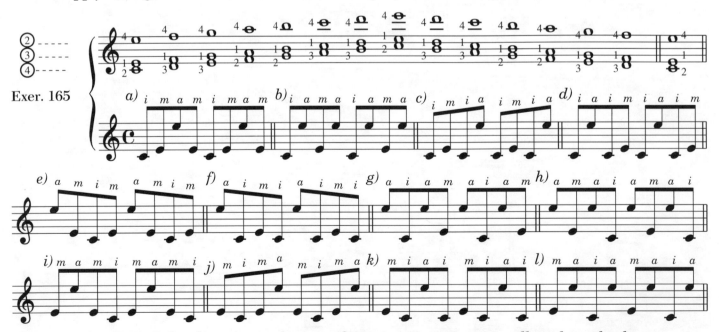

Exer. 165

The instructions given for the previous lesson referring to Exercise 164, will apply to this lesson.

Four-Note Arpeggio on Two Non-Adjacent Strings, with Separation Between Index-Middle and Middle-Annular Fingers

248. — Apply the left hand formula given for Exercise 166 to the mechanisms that accompany it, carefully maintaining the stability of the hand, the flexibility of the fingers, and firmness in striking the strings.

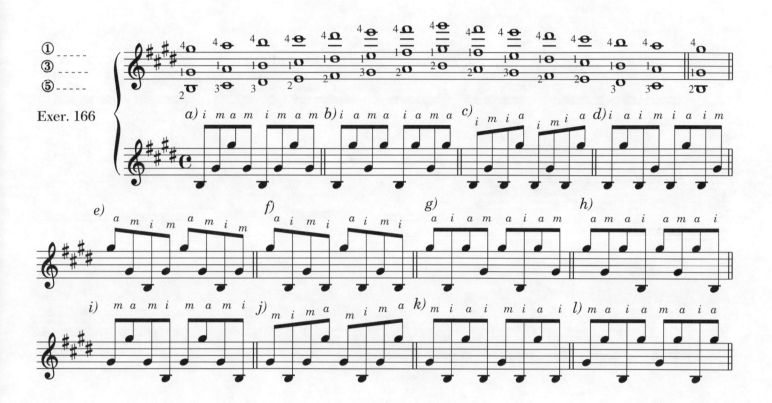

249. — Work on Study XXVII.

Specific Instructions for Study XXVII

[347.] — Arpeggios on non-adjacent strings without the use of the thumb.

a) *Apoyando* is appropriate for this arpeggio.

b) Of primary importance is the reliability of the right hand and the positions of the left hand, while avoiding *unwanted glissandi* that tend to be produced on the 5th string during changes of position.

c) The notes corresponding to the annular finger, which plays the melody apoyando, as well as those of the inner voices which offer special interest (harmonic and melodic) should be brought out with the intensity required by its expressive intent.

d) Assure good sound on each note and continuity of the arpeggio while joining together the phrases of each period paying attention to the indicated dynamics.

As with other Studies in this book, this piece's technical character is combined with an emotional grounding which should not be disdained by anyone wishing to obtain the greatest possible benefit from its practice.

Study XXVII
(Nocturne)

69

250. — Having practiced together to this point, all the principal formulas of the arpeggio with regard to the order of and distance between the fingers, the pupil should distribute his work in such a way that he is able to practice the different mechanisms of each formula on a daily basis, varying them successively so that the fingers are always disposed to execute everything with equal facility.

<h1 style="text-align:center">LESSON 90</h1>

<h2 style="text-align:center">Apoyando and Tirando. Chords on Three Adjacent Strings</h2>

251. — Apply right hand mechanisms a), b), c), d), and e) to the accompanying left hand formula.

a) All chords on adjacent strings are necessarily struck *tirando*.

b) The *tirando* articulation of the chord should be followed by an *apoyando* stroke with the annular finger. Be attentive to the simultaneity of the notes of the chord and the equality of volume between the notes struck *tirando* and those which the annular finger strikes *apoyando*[1].

c) The middle and annular fingers simultaneously pluck *tirando*; the index finger plays *apoyando*.[2]

d) The annular finger strikes *apoyando* and the index and middle fingers *tirando*.

e) All fingers play *tirando*.

---

1 Likewise, practice this formula *tirando*.
2 See previous footnote.

The following left hand formulas, to which the same preceding right hand mechanisms can be applied, will offer the pupil variety in the practice of plucking the strings.

Exercise 167(b)

Exercise 167(c)

Exercise 167(d)

252. — Work on Study XXVIII.

Specific Instructions for Study XXVIII

[348.] — Alternating chords and single notes.

a) Take care that the notes of the chords are struck at the same time and that the ones in between, played by either the *annular* or *index* fingers, have the same intensity as the chords, in order to obtain the required continuity in the voices to which they belong.

b) Maintain the position of the left hand (See Book I, § 100) with the force necessary so that the vibration of the notes does not stop before their respective values have terminated.

c) The changes of position in the fingers between some of the chords contained in bars 1 to 4 and 23 to 31 should be performed with sufficient lightness and precision so that there results no change in the evenness of the tempo.

d) The single notes that follow the chords should be struck tirando to avoid stopping the note of the chord played on the next string.

e) The bracket ([) to the left of two or more simultaneous notes (final measure) indicates that they are to be played at the same time by sliding the *thumb* in one motion over the strings where the notes are found.

STUDY XXVIII

(Harvest Song)

TEMPO I.

scherzando

LESSON 91

Same Practice on Four Adjacent Strings

253. — Apply the indicated right hand mechanisms to the following left hand formula.

a) All fingers play *tirando*.

b) The index and middle fingers will play *tirando;* the annular, *apoyando*[1].

c) *Apoyando* for the *annular* and *tirando* for the *index* and *middle*.

d) Only the index plays *apoyando*[2].

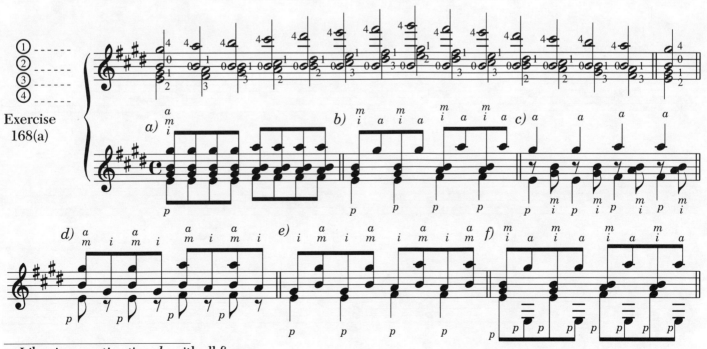

Exercise 168(a)

---

1 Likewise, practice *tirando* with all fingers.

2 See previous footnote.

e) All fingers *tirando.*

f) As in mechanism b), only the *annular* finger plays *apoyando.* At the same time, pluck the open sixth string with the thumb.

Exercise 168(b)

The following left hand formula can give variety to these mechanisms.

254. — Work on Study XXIX.

Specific Instructions for Study XXIX

[349.] — Simultaneous use of thumb-index, and middle-annular fingers.

a) Bring out the notes corresponding to the *index* finger since they belong to the principal voice.

b) Strive to obtain and maintain the richest sonority possible from the first chord on, avoiding not only *unwanted glissandi,* but also the interruption of sound when moving the hand from one position to another.

c) This is to be performed slowly with gravity so that the modality, ambience, and noble Incan spirituality which gives it character appears vigorously reflected in the rhythm and beauty of its melody.

Study XXIX
(Vidala)

LESSON 92

Same Practice on Non-Adjacent Strings for the Middle and Index Fingers

255. — Apply the right hand mechanisms to the following left hand formula that accompanies them.

a) *Tirando.*

b) Be careful that the distance between the strings struck by the index and middle fingers does not cause insecurity nor lack of simultaneity in striking the notes of the chord. The *annular* finger will also play *tirando.* Avoid jumping about with the hand.

c) The *annular* finger can also play this mechanism *apoyando.*

d) No finger should play *apoyando.*

e) No finger plays *apoyando.*

The following left hand formula can also be applied to these mechanisms.

256. — Work on Study XXX.

[350.] — Simultaneous use of the *thumb, middle,* and *annular* fingers alternating successively with the *index* finger.

Old Gallician folk song. The melody in this version consists of four phrases of a different number of bars in each, preceded and linked by two contrasting bars.

a) Bring out the notes played by the *annular* finger since they are those of the melody, being careful that the notes played by the *index* finger do not interrupt the resonance of those that have been played by the *thumb.*

b) Measures 1, 2, 7, 8, 13, 14, 19, 20, 25, 26, and 27 should be played quietly since they constitute the more distant plane over which the melody is brought out.

Study XXX
(Alalá - Galician Song)

LESSON 93

Combined Chords on Four Strings.
Index-Middle and Middle-Annular on Non-Adjacent Strings

257. — Apply the present left hand formula to the following right hand mechanisms, according to the instructions given in Lesson 92 in regard to Exercise 173.

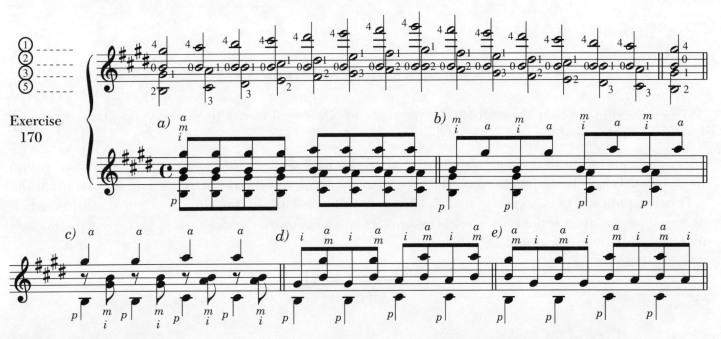

Exercise 170

The annular finger plays *apoyando* on mechanisms b) and c); the *index* finger plays *apoyando* only on mechanisms d) and e).

LESSON 94

Combined Chords on Four Strings.
Index-Middle and Middle-Annular on Non-Adjacent Strings

258. — Proceed with these chords as in the previous lessons, trying to place the left hand in a position that assures good sound from the strings and that the plucking is firm and secure in each right hand formula.

Exercise 171

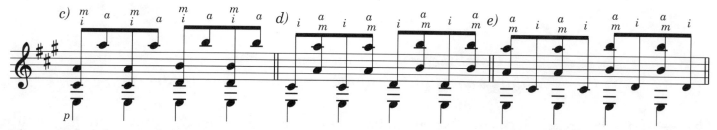

The annular finger plays *apoyando* on formulas b) and c); the index finger plays *tirando* on every formula.

259. — Work on Study XXXI.

Specific Instructions for Study XXXI

[351.] — Basque *canción-danza* from the province of Navarra. Four-note chords. Simultaneous use of the *thumb, index, middle,* and *annular* fingers.

a) Pay close attention to the meter and rhythm, within the indicated tempo. b) Strive for reliability and that all chords are struck together. c) The fingers of the left hand should be placed on the strings at the frets corresponding to each position all at the same time. d) The rhythm should not be disturbed when changing positions with the fingers. e) Measures 29 and 31 require special care. f) Bring out the melody observing the given dynamics.

Study XXXI
(Zorztico)

Movement of the Thumb on Simultaneous Chords of Three and Four Notes

Exercise 172

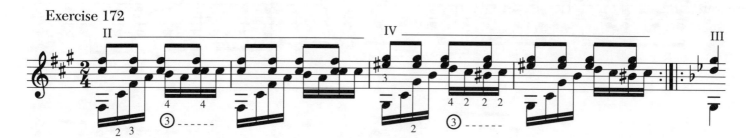

260. — Heed the action of the thumb, playing in such a way that its movements always seem independent from the rest of the hand. Remember that in more frequent movements, this finger should not move too far from the string to avoid creating a harsh sound as a result of attacking the string from too far away.

Likewise, pay attention to the clarity of the notes and the flexibility of the left hand when moving from the second to the third measure and from the fourth back to the first measure at the repeat.

Practice transposing to the corresponding key of different consecutive quintuplets as well.

Exercise 173

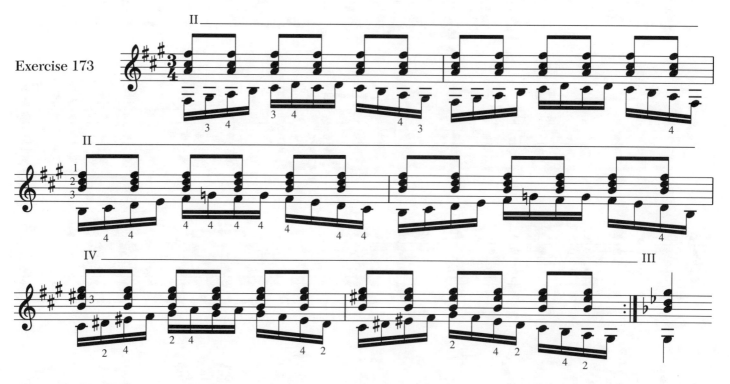

Take heed of the remarks referred to in the previous exercise striving to avoid the small bounce in the right hand wrist four note chords can create.

LESSON 96

Three-Note Arpeggios
Playing Simultaneously with the Thumb on the First Note of Each Arpeggio

261. — The natural position of the right hand over the strings leaves the index, middle, and annular fingers disposed to strike the strings from the direction of the basses to the trebles respectively; thus,

ascending arpeggios of three notes over three adjacent or non-adjacent strings will be struck with the fingering *i-m-a;* and the descending ones with the inverse fingering, *a-m-i.*

262. — Since the *apoyando* gives more stability to the hand and greater intensity and volume to the notes, in general slow arpeggios will preferably be executed *apoyando.*

However, the duration, intensity, and velocity of the notes will require, in some cases, a change of stroke from rest to free and vice versa.

263. — The sound of a note played on a given string will be interrupted the moment a finger plays *apoyando* on the next higher string. Thus, when one of the fingers, index, middle, or annular, has to play a string next to one attacked by the thumb, it strikes it *tirando.*

264. — In an arpeggio it is always necessary to bring out a given note and when it does not coincide with a note struck by the thumb on an adjacent string, it is played *apoyando.*

265. — The arpeggio, although written conventionally in groups of successive notes of partial value, should be executed in rapid movements as if the real value of the notes lasts the total duration of the arpeggio. And, as it is not possible with the guitar to use the pedal that so ingeniously resolves this situation on the piano leaving the strings to freely vibrate, one must attain this effect with the fingers' avoiding any contact with the strings that could inhibit the duration of the sound.

266. — With respect to this, rapidly *ascending* arpeggios will be played *tirando* so that no finger will make contact with notes already sounding.

267. — In *descending* arpeggios, since the rest stroke on the next string does not silence the previous note, it will be possible to play *apoyando,* if one wishes, with the three fingers corresponding to the notes of the arpeggio.

The notes of the arpeggio which coincide with the corresponding bass line of the thumb will only be able to be played with the middle, index, or annular fingers *apoyando* when they are found on strings not adjacent to the bass.

Exercise 174

Practice formulas a), b), c), d), e), and f) without pause and combine with the following exercise:

Exercise 175

The distance between the *thumb* and the *rest of the fingers* should not be cause for any unevenness of movement of the fingers.

LESSON 97

Three-Note Arpeggio Playing Simultaneously with the Thumb on the First and Second Notes of Each Arpeggio

Exercise 176

Follow the same instructions given for the exercises in the previous lesson being careful to make precise movements with the thumb and evenness in the arpeggio.

Exercise 177

LESSON 98

Three-Note Arpeggio Playing Simultaneously with the Thumb on the First and Third Notes of Each Arpeggio

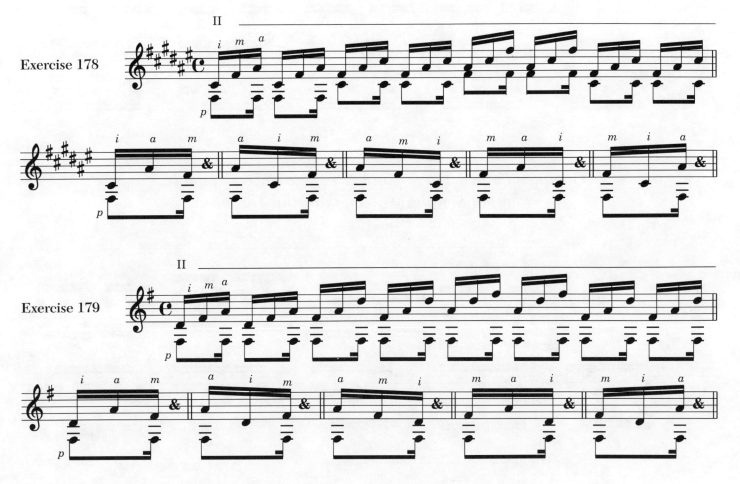

Practice following the instructions given for the exercises in the previous lesson.

LESSON 99

Three-Note Arpeggios Playing Simultaneously with the Thumb on Each Note of the Arpeggio

Practice in the manner described for the previous exercises, developing the speed of the thumb, without altering the balance of the hand.

Exercise 181

LESSON 100

Complementary Three-Note Arpeggio Patterns while Playing Simultaneously with the Thumb

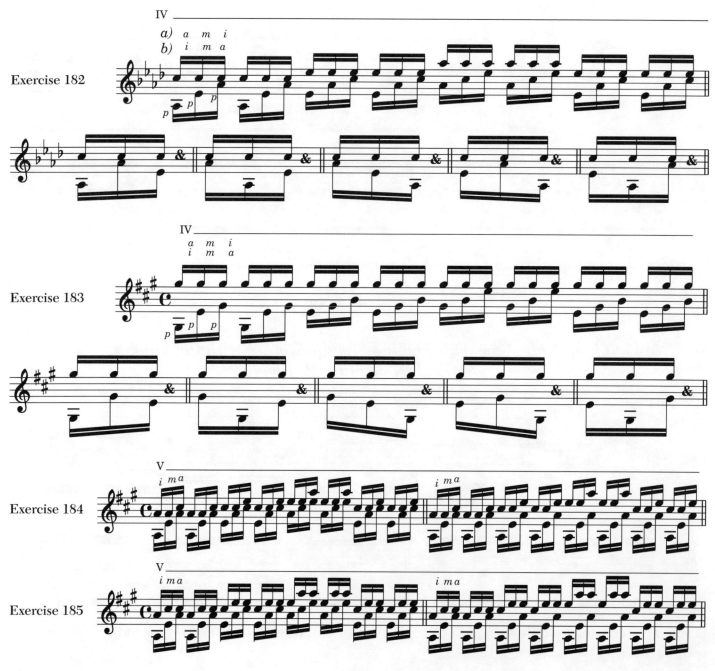

Exercise 182

Exercise 183

Exercise 184

Exercise 185

Exercise 186

Follow the instructions given in lesson 96, paying particular attention to the action of the *thumb*.

268. — Work on Study XXXII.

Specific Instructions for Study XXXII

[352.] — Three-note arpeggio with simultaneous use of the thumb.

a) In arpeggios of continual regularity, be careful with the simultaneity of the bass, whose expression depends on the thumb.

b) Play *apoyando* whenever using either *i, m,* or *a* against the thumb, except when on contiguous strings.

c) Do not interrupt the sound when moving from one string to the next.

d) Protect the sonority of the arpeggio by allowing each string to continue resonating.

e) The fusion of the sonority of each arpeggio with the melodic expression of the bass will prevent the seeming monotony of this Study, a poetic concept of singular interest and emotion.

Study XXXII

(Nocturne)

Adagio sostenuto (♩.=54)

LESSON 101

Slurs in Fixed Position. Exercises of Resistance and Motion to Develop the Strength and Independence of the Fingers of the Left Hand

269. — Nothing will succeed in developing the necessary strength or independence in the fingers of the left hand as the practice of slurs in fixed position, if they are worked with diligence and attention. They are gymnastic exercises that should be practiced as the groundwork for flexibility in the joints and elasticity and strength in the muscles of the hands and fingers. Any abrupt or forced movements in the fingers or the arm, instead of increasing and facilitating the possibilities of the hand, tense-up the muscles and disturb the motion of the fingers.

Each exercise will develop strength and independence of a given finger in relation to any other finger and across all distances presented by the strings as a result of their disposition.

To ensure their usefulness, practice them in the following manner:

1st — Position each finger or fingers that are to remain fixed on one or more given strings corresponding to the "X"-notes, and press as perpendicularly as possible during the entire repetition of the slurred notes produced by the other fingers.

2nd — Lift the finger that is to produce the slur if ascending, bending it[1] forcefully as great a distance from the string as possible trying not to disturb the finger that is holding the "X" note.

3rd — Lift the finger again to this distance and let it fall with force on the string and fret on which the slurred note is produced.

4th — Then, to create the descending slur, pull the same finger off with force, letting it come to rest on the next string.

5th — Return the finger to its natural position, repeating the same movements.

6th — The fingers that remain fixed as well as those which produce the slurred notes will concentrate their force in the last phalange leaving the rest of the hand in repose.

The difficulty increases as the distance between the fingers becomes greater and especially when this distance coincides between fingers 3 and 4 because of the anatomical properties of the third finger and the shortness of the fourth. Muscular weariness or fatigue that is found in the fingers at first (especially in the thumb because of its constant resistance at the back of the neck), should not deter one from his work. It is advisable to spend a minimum of 30 seconds per day on each slur formula. Resting the hand after experiencing fatigue will give the fingers very beneficial residual strength and independence.

270. — Slurs with fingers *2* and *3*, emphasizing the gradual spread between them and finger *1*.

---

1 [Ed.: ie., toward the palm.]

The right forearm and hand can rest on the lower bout of the guitar while the left hand practices these exercises alone. The "X"-notes are silent. Position the first finger at the first fret of the sixth string and practice the slur on each string very slowly and deliberately for at least 30 seconds.

271. — Slurs with fingers *2* and *4* progressively increasing the spread between them and finger *1*.

Articulate finger *4* with force practicing at different quadruplets.

272. — Slurred notes for fingers *3* and *4* with a gradual spread between them and finger *1*.

Practice like the previous exercise articulating finger *4* deliberately.

273. — Slurred notes for fingers *3* and *4* with a gradual spread between them and finger *2*.

Practice as in the preceding exercises articulating finger *4* with force.

274. — Slurred notes for fingers *1* and *3* with a gradual spread between them and finger *2*.

Articulate finger *3* with force.

275. — Slurred notes for fingers *2* and *4* with gradual spread from finger *3*.

Articulate finger *4* with force, practicing at different quadruplets.

276. — Slurs for fingers *1* and *2* progressively increasing the spread between them and finger *3*.

Articulate finger *2* with force.

277. — Slurs for fingers *3* and *2*, with a gradual spread between them and finger *4*.

Practice raising finger *3* as high as possible and only on those formulas the disposition of the fingers of the pupil permit.

278. — Slurs with fingers *3* and *1* with a gradual spread between them and finger *4*.

Practice as in the previous exercise, paying attention to the difficulty of the slur caused by the position and size of finger *4*.

279. — Slurs with fingers *4* and *1* with a gradual spread between them and fingers *3* and *2*.

Exercise 196

Repeat at several quadruplets articulating finger *4* with force.

LESSON 102

Complement to the Previous Lesson. Inversion of the Same Distances

280. — Slurs for fingers *3* and *2* with a gradual spread between them and finger *1*.

Exercise 197

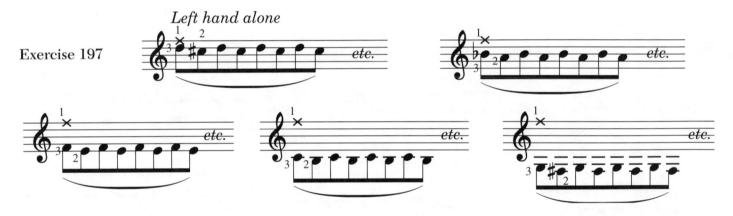

Practice slowly at different quadruplets articulating finger *3* with force.

281. — Slurs for fingers *4* and *2* progressively increasing the spread between them and finger *1*.

Exercise 198

Practice as in the previous exercise, articulating finger *4*.

282. — Slurs for fingers *4* and *3* with a gradual spread between them and finger *2*.

Practice at whatever distances the reach and flexibility of the hand permit.

283. — Slurs for fingers *3* and *1* progressively increasing the spread between them and finger *2*.

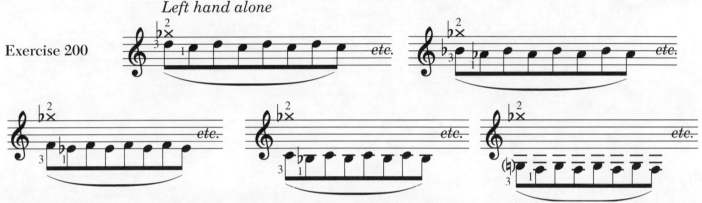

Practice at different quadruplets articulating finger *3* with force.

284. — Slurs for fingers *4* and *3* progressively increasing the spread between them and finger *1*.

Practice as in the previous exercise articulating finger *4* with force.

285. — Slurs for fingers *4* and *2* with a gradual spread between them and finger *3*.

Practice at distances that the hand of the pupil can reach, without forcing too much.

286. — Slurs for fingers *3* and *2* progressively increasing the spread between them and finger *4*.

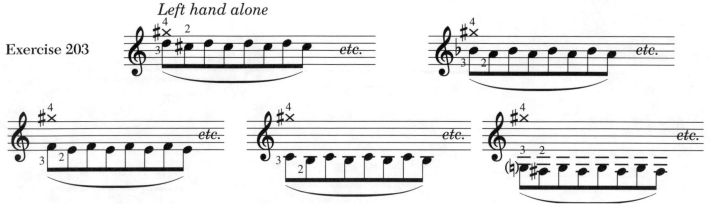

Also practice relative to the extent permitted by the hand.

287. — Slurs for fingers *4* and *1* with a gradual spread between them and finger *3*.

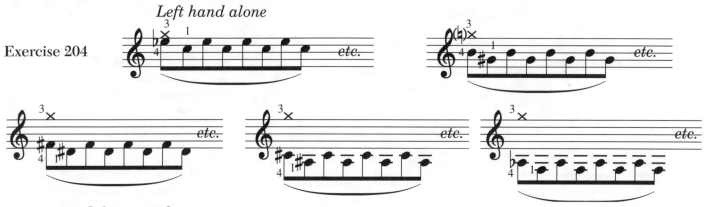

Bear in mind the same directions.

288. — Slurs for fingers *2* and *1*, increasing the spread between them and finger *3*.

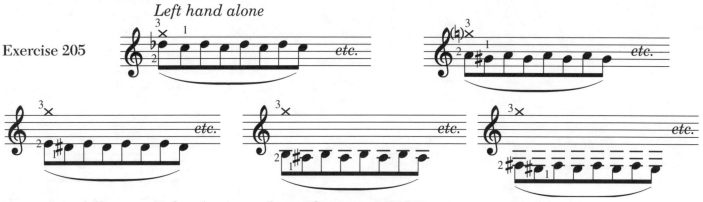

Practice in different quadruplets articulating finger 2 with force.

289. — Slurs for fingers *4* and *1*, progressively increasing the spread between them and fingers *2* and *3*.

Practice on the strings and quadruplets that the hand of the pupil will permit without forcing too much.

LESSON 103

Slurs Combined with Notes Struck Along the Length of the String

290. — Chromatic progression of ascending and descending slurs on each string.

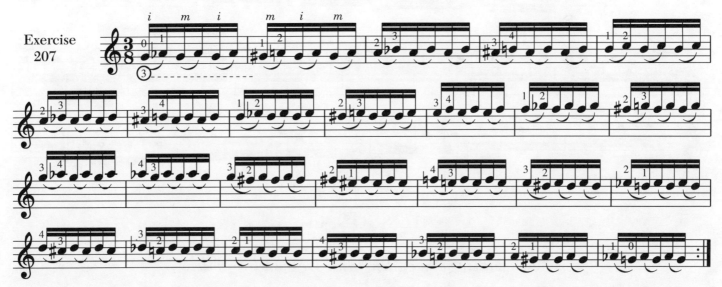

Repeat (transposed) on the second, first, fourth, and fifth strings, keeping the same arrangement of frets and fingers. Practice slowly, going faster once the coordination of both hands is achieved.

291. — Inversion of the previous slurs.

Practice in the same way as the previous exercise.

292. — Diatonic progression of ascending and descending slurs on each string.

Follow the same instructions given for the two previous exercises, being careful to achieve clarity in the slurred notes, especially when the fingers perform in an open position.

293. — Inversion of the same exercise.

Follow the directions referred to in the previous exercise.

LESSON 104

Alternating Ascending and Descending Slurs

294. — *Ascending* and *descending* progression.

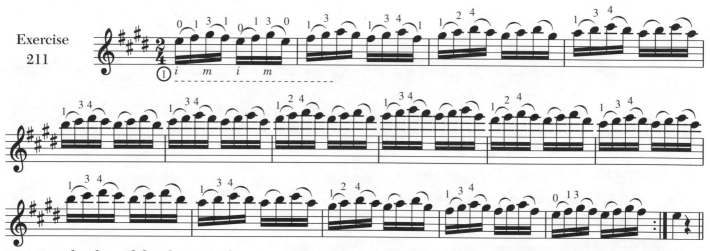

Practice slowly and firmly on each string, going faster once the coordination of both hands is achieved.

295. — Complement to the previous exercise.

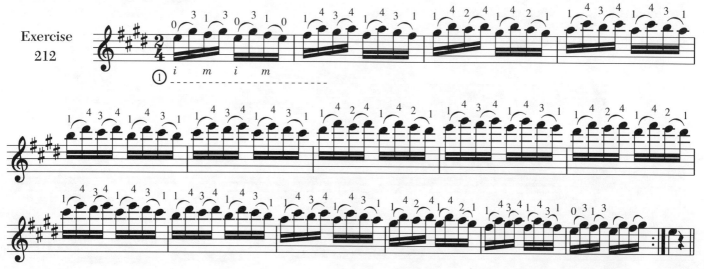

Practice in the same way and with the same care as the preceding exercise.

296. — Ascending and descending three-note slurs.

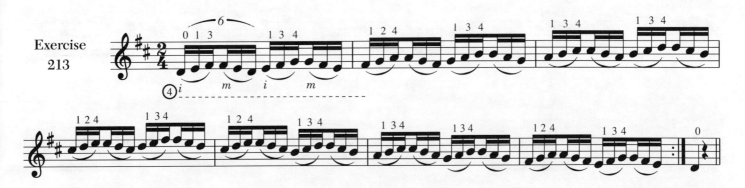

Strike only the first note of each triplet paying attention to the intensity and evenness of the three notes. Repeat on the third, second, first, and fifth strings.

297. — Work on Study XXXIII.

Specific Instructions for Study XXXIII

[353.] — Slurs

a) *Slurred* notes should be played by the left hand in such a way that they sound as though they were produced by the right hand with an effect of lightness and smooth continuity.

b) The slurs in measures 6 and 8 require special care where the first note encountered in the bar is far from the nut and the second note is on the same string open.

c) Likewise, be careful with the evenness of the notes of the chromatic scale (bars 13 and 14) as well as the agility and strength of the slurs in bars 15 and 16.

d) Although at first it will be useful to work the left hand fingers slowly and with force, later it will be necessary to practice with the greatest velocity possible without sacrificing clarity.

Study XXXIII

96

LESSON 105

Appoggiaturas. Simple Ascending and Descending Appoggiaturas

298. — All who know music theory know that the word appoggiatura means a supporting note without effective value that anticipates a principal note of given value, both of which have the same intensity. The appoggiatura takes its value from the note it affects and is *brief* or *short* when it is represented with a stem and flag crossed by a small slash; in this case it is also given the name *acciaccatura* and is performed as quickly as possible.

The word *appoggiatura* has the same meaning in terms of guitar technique. Aguado, in his method (Lesson 27, § 132), adds that *"its practice is like a two-note slur, but performed with great promptness."*

Appoggiaturas can be *simple, double,* and by *glissando* or *slide*.

The *simple appoggiatura* is generally found at a distance of a whole-step or half-step above or below the principal note. In *ascending* appoggiaturas, the small note is struck leaving the finger to fall on the following note. *Descending* appoggiaturas are performed striking the small note and immediately pulling the finger off the string so the following note will sound. The movement for each appoggiatura has to be short, as though one had the intention of playing two slurred notes at the same time.

299. — "Simple" *Ascending* appoggiatura.

Practice slowly, allowing the finger that has to produce the principal note to come down rapidly and firmly, striving to achieve the same intensity for each note.

300. — "Simple" *Descending* appoggiatura.

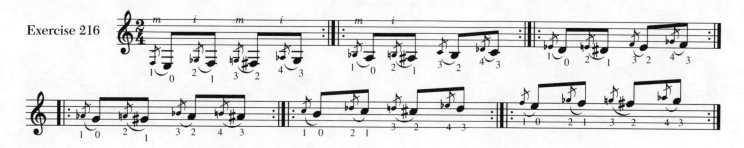

97

Exercise 217

Practice in the same way as the preceding exercises, pulling the finger off the string firmly at the moment the first note is produced, with the intention of giving equal intensity to the principal note.

301. — Work on Study XXXIV.

Specific Instructions for Study XXXIV

[354.] — Three-note arpeggio in different orders and accentuation.

a) Bring out the notes marked with the sign (>) above or below.

b) The slur of the appoggiaturas should be rapid and deliberate, articulated by the tip joint of the finger.

c) Assure precise meter and rhythmic accentuation.

The Bulería, characterized by the Andalusian dance style and rhythmic syncopation, must be animated by a particular indefinable grace that is the soul of its character and style.

STUDY XXXIV

(In the manner of a Bulerías)

LESSON 106

Double Appoggiaturas

302. — The *double appoggiatura* consists of two notes. When *ascending*, the first of the two notes is struck and the fingers corresponding to the second note and the principal note are immediately allowed to fall successively onto the string, without plucking more than the first note, taking care that they stop the string precisely next to the fret.

For the *descending* double appoggiatura, the three fingers that correspond to their three notes are positioned at the same time; the first is struck without any other plucking, and immediately the finger that stops that note and the next finger are successively pulled off the string to sound the second and third notes. Generally, at first, all the force tends to be borne by the finger of the principal note; but it shouldn't be that way; in any case, one must reinforce the first note, thus avoiding the tendency of the hand and arm to pull toward the rear. At the beginning, one must become reconciled to a small sound, while the notes are heard with clarity. (See Aguado's *Method*, lesson 29, § 135).

303. — *Ascending* and *descending* "double appoggiatura."

The *ascending* appoggiatura should be practiced allowing the fingers that correspond to the second note of the appoggiatura and the principal note[1] to fall rapidly with force, emphasizing the power of the finger that corresponds to this last note. Position the fingers that correspond to the notes of the *descending* appoggiatura and principal note, successively pulling off the first two with force while striving to accent the third note which corresponds to the principal note.

---

1 [Ed.: Original reads: "...the fingers that correspond to the two notes of the appoggiatura and the principle note."]

LESSON 107

Appoggiatura by Slide or Glissando

304. — This appoggiatura consists of executing the two notes by means of a glissando or slide that moves from the first note and finishes on the principal note. When the appoggiatura is short, (of the type known as *acciaccatura)*, the slide should be made rapidly, emphasizing the pressure on the string while moving to the principal note.

Exercise 220

Practice making the slide as rapidly as possible, accenting the principal note.

305. — When said appoggiatura is one of those that is given half the value of the following note, the slide will be made without increasing pressure when moving to the principal note and after giving the first its appropriate length. In both cases it will be performed with flexibility avoiding constriction in the hand or arm.

Exercise 221

Practice the slide accenting the first note and giving to each one half the value of the principal note.

LESSON 108

Mordents. Simple Ascending Mordent

306. — The mordent consists of a double appoggiatura, ascending and descending, whose first note is equal in pitch to the principal note.

There are three types of mordents: the simple mordent, the double mordent, and the turn.[1]

The simple mordent consists of two notes, the first of which is the same as the principal note, and the second, although with exceptions, is generally found at a distance of a whole-step or half-step above or below it. In the first case — ascending mordent — , the first two notes are performed like an ascending slur and then the finger that produced the second note is forcefully pulled off the string so that the principal note is heard with clarity and intensity. These two combined slurs have to be performed without interruption, as quickly as possible.

---

1 [Ed.: Pujol uses the term "circular mordent."]

Exercise 222

Strive to achieve clarity and evenness of sound, always accenting the principal note.

Exercise 223

307. — Work on Study XXXV.

Specific Instructions for Study XXXV

[355.] — Ascending mordent.

a) Tune the sixth string one octave below the open fourth string.

b) Although the notes corresponding to the thumb or other finger generally appear below the principal note of the mordent, they should be struck simultaneously with the first note as though written in the following form:

Even though this would be the correct indication of the value of the mordent, tradition has made it customary in the other notation.

c) So that the mordent is not confused with the triplet, its execution should be made rapidly with an accent on its principal note.

d) Be attentive to the fingering of both hands, observing the speed, clarity, and accent of the mordents and following the tempo and dynamic indications so that the composition obtains the vibrancy of spirit that makes it come to life.

Study XXXV

Allegretto grazioso (♩.=76)

Come prima

LESSON 109

"Simple" Descending Mordent

308. — In the second case — descending mordents — the fingers that correspond to the first two notes are positioned on the strings and the first is pulled off the string after it has been sounded so that the second note is clearly heard, allowing the finger corresponding to the principal note to fall back on the string immediately. Both slurs should be performed without interruption and with such promptness as though they were simultaneous with the principal note.

Exercise 224

Exercise 225

Strive for clarity and evenness of sound, always accenting the principal note.

309. — Work on Study XXXVI.

Specific Instructions for Study XXXVI

[356.] — Descending mordent.

a) To confirm what was expressed in Study XXXV with respect to the simultaneity between the thumb and the first note of the mordent, but here working on a piece written at a tempo slower than the one before, the pupil will encounter in this Study the true notation of the note values that in the customary system would have been notated thus:

b) The principal note should be accented in all mordents. For the double mordents (see Lesson 110, § 310) found in measures 19, 21, and 31, be especially careful since the accent is more difficult to make.

c) Pay attention to the interpretive indications that are given, particularly the progression contained in bars 22, 23, and 24 where the emotional expression of the composition climaxes.

Study XXXVI

LESSON 110

Ascending and Descending "Double" Mordent

310. — The double mordent is composed of three small notes clustered about one note. They can be ascending or descending. In the first case, there are ascending slurs, those that move from the first to the second note and from there to the third; and descending slurs, those which go from the third small note to the principal note. The four notes should be performed without interruption and with great rapidity, accenting the last note without constricting the arm or hand.

Exercise 226

311. — In the descending double mordent, there are descending slurs that join the first note to the second and from there to the third; the ascending slur is that which joins this last note to the principal note. The four notes should be performed promptly, without interruption, accenting the principal note without encountering any constriction in the hand or arm.

Exercise 227

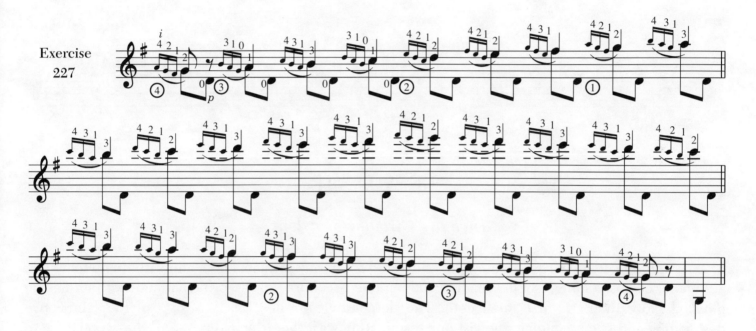

312. — The double mordent is called *mixed* when one of the slurs that comprises it is substituted by a glissando.

When ascending, the finger which plays the first note slides forcefully to the fret where the second note is produced so that this note is heard with the same clarity as though it were slurred.

Exercise 228

When descending, the slide is produced between the third and principal note of the mordent. Take care that the bass does not over-power the slurred treble voice.

LESSON 111

Turn or "Circular Mordent"

313. — This mordent consists of four notes clustered about one principal note and with them, four slurs are made; one ascending, two descending and another ascending to the principal note without having plucked more than the first small note. The descending mordent also consists of four slurs; two descending and two ascending, the last one terminating with the principal note. All these notes are to be performed with flexibility without tightening the fingers too much and are to be heard with clarity, although at first they won't have too much sound. It happens that so much force when pulling each finger away to produce the descending slurs will naturally oblige the hand to move away; it is necessary to avoid this defect, and to try to carry the fingers that are making the slurs parallel to the frets, though without forcing them; good practice will strengthen them.

LESSON 112

Extended Appoggiaturas and Slurs

314. — There is also an appoggiatura of several chromatic or diatonic notes in ascending or descending succession. They are performed like very fast slurs, always striving to accentuate the principal note.

Exercise 232

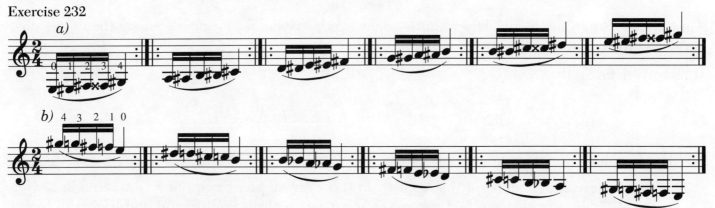

Proceed as with the double appoggiatura exercises (Lesson 106) accenting the principal note.

Since this exercise reviews formulas a) and b) of the previous exercise, practice joining the group of ascending slurs with the descending slurs without interruption, striving for the greatest possible evenness of sound.

Exercise 234

Try to join the slurred notes so that the movement from one string to the next is not obvious.

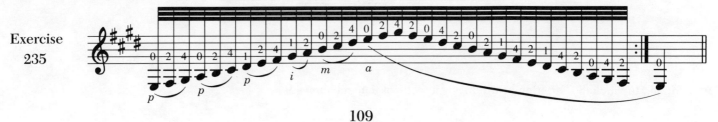

109

Exercise 236

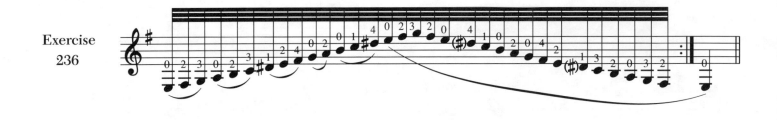

Exercise 237

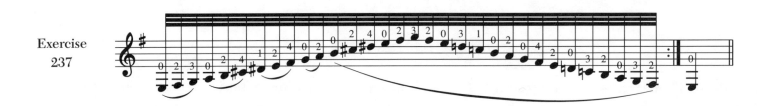

Join the ascending slurs by plucking with the right hand, striving for evenness among the descending slurs that are executed by the left hand alone.

315. — Work on Study XXXVII.

Specific Instructions for Study XXXVII

[357.] — Extended double mordents and slurs.

a) The double descending mordent that appears in this Study is similar to the turn treated in Lesson 111. It differs from it in that the first two notes are struck with the right hand and have a different rhythmic value. Try to give the slurred notes their correct value, being certain they are heard with the necessary power, clarity, and nuance.

b) Be particularly careful with the rhythm, phrasing, and accentuation of the notes indicated with the accent mark (>) since it is this which gives character to the composition.

c) The melody should be brought out in an expressive manner from bar 13 to 21 taking care that the passages of slurred notes, like those in bars 16, 17, and 21, do not interrupt the continuity of the melody.

d) Pay attention to the evenness of the slurred notes and the thumb strokes made in the manner of an Andalusian *falseta*[1], contained in measure 27.

e) The chords in bars 34 and 35 should be played with the thumb.

f) The end of bar 35 requires sureness, speed, and decisiveness.

This is the Bolero, a Spanish dance of the 18th century. It is not enough to simply interpret it according to strict rhythm; it requires warm-bloodedness and a feeling of intense noble grace for its performance.

---

1 [Ed.: ie., the melodic variation heard during a *toque* of flamenco music]

For the purpose of correct page turns, this page left intentionally blank

Study XXXVII
Bolero

Allegretto rítmico (♩=88)

113

LESSON 113

Vibrato

316. — The left hand is able to contribute to the prolongation (more or less limited) of the sound of one or more notes and give them greater intensity by means of vibrato. (See "Temblor," Book One, § 228).

Having a finger in position on a given string at a given fret, for example the second finger on the first string, fifth fret (a), and making a motion with this finger left to right without diminishing the pressure exerted on the string at the fret, the sound will be prolonged by small undulations. This effect is that which is indicated by the word *vibrato*.

317. — To produce it the way it should be, one must agitate the finger at the precise moment the string is struck, taking advantage of the first vibrations (the most intense ones), without losing in this way the same degree of force on the string as existed at the very beginning. These motions should not be too lively nor too stressful on the wrist. Some performers practice vibrato lifting the thumb from the neck, a defect which should be avoided so that balance can be maintained. (See the *Method* of Aguado, Lesson 44, § 188 to § 191).

Good execution of vibrato depends less on the pressure of the fingers than the way in which it is practiced. It is necessary to rest the last phalange of the finger that produces the vibrato on the string paying attention that the hand's own inertia sustains and prolongs the vibrations better than the excessive force that the arm pretends to give.

318. — Vibrato can be found on each string, at each fret, but, since the length of the string is reduced above the twelfth fret and the vibrations of the string are less wide, the effect of vibrato is less noticeable.

319. — Since vibrato depends on the oscillatory movements of the hand, it is not possible to use vibrato on a single stopped note with a given finger when another finger or fingers are in the act of stopping strings. However, it is possible to use vibrato on two or more notes at the same time provided the hand is not immobilized by the barré.

320. — The expressive effect of vibrato which so enriches the performance of the guitarist should be used opportunely and in moderation if one wishes to avoid mannerisms and bad taste.

321. — Notes that should be played with vibrato are written with special signs in some old guitar tablatures (see Book One, §§ 134-160). Present literature does not indicate it, leaving it up to the free interpretation of the performer. In general, those notes belonging to lyrical melodies will receive vibrato whenever possible, above all if expressive sentiments of sensitivity and emotion are embraced.

The pupil should try to use vibrato on the preceding notes, applying it (in agreement with the teacher) to those melodic notes susceptible to vibrato that are within his grasp.

LESSON 114

Octave Harmonics

322. — Octave harmonics are artificial harmonics, taking advantage of a node midway between the bridge and the fret in which the string is stopped.

323. — If we consider that the point which coincides with the fretwire that separates frets XII and XIII is that which divides the length of the string into two halves producing a harmonic one octave above each open string, we deduce that the same string stopped at the first fret will give its octave harmonic at the division between frets XIII-XIV. Stopping the string at the second fret, the harmonic is found at the division between frets XIV-XV and so on in the same way; that is, *the octave harmonic of a note stopped on a given string will be found exactly above the fretwire that is the same number of frets from the twelfth fret toward the bridge that the finger stopping the note is from the nut.*

Table of Octave Harmonics

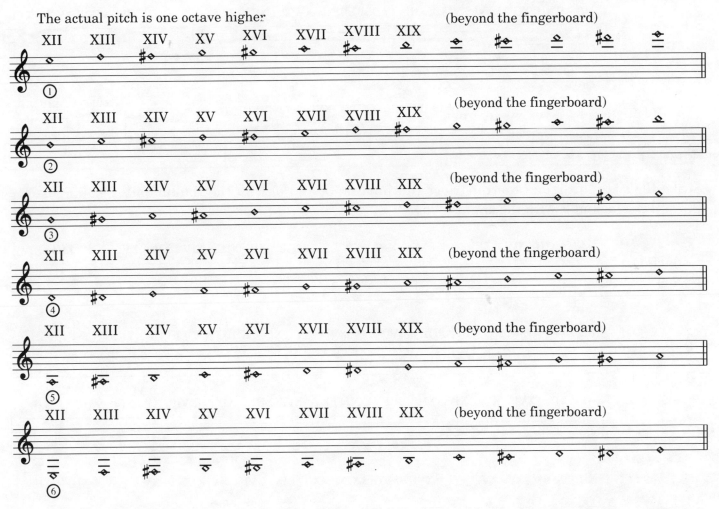

324. — Since in these cases the fingers of the left hand are occupied with their normal proceedings, it is necessary that the fingers of the right hand perform two jobs simultaneously; that of lightly touching the string and of plucking the harmonic. To do this, the index finger of the right hand is extended in such a way that the inside part of the tip joint[1] is lightly positioned on the string at the point of the division of the fret corresponding to the harmonic, simultaneously plucking tirando with the annular finger.

1 [Ed.: i.e., the pad of the fingertip.]

115

325. — In the same way, these harmonics can be performed by plucking them with the thumb. The index likewise proceeds, extending itself to make contact with the string at the precise point where the node is formed; the thumb simultaneously strikes the string bending its last phalange toward the palm of the hand, diagonally to the plane of the strings.

Strike the sixth, fifth, and fourth strings (formulas a, b, and c) with the thumb and remaining strings (formulas d, e, and f) with the annular finger.

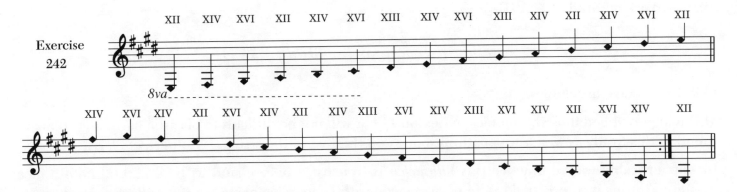

Play these four exercises using only the annular finger.

LESSON 115

Octave Harmonics While Simultaneously Using the Thumb

326. — The harmonics that are played with the *annular* finger allow simultaneous plucking with the *thumb.* In such cases, the thumb, following the displacement of the right hand, plays by articulating its last phalange toward the palm as in normal performance, without obstructing the action of the *index* or *annular* fingers.

117

Specific Instructions for Study XXVIII

[358.] — Octave harmonics.

a) Having practiced those harmonics in Lesson 114, it will not be difficult to play the harmonics that are found in this Study as well as the natural sounds on the rest of the strings with perfect clarity.

b) The advisable way to practice this *Villancico* is to learn it beforehand with all natural notes; once mastered in this way, proceed in the performance with harmonics being careful with the simultaneity of both hands.

Study XXXVIII

(from a 16th century *villancico*)

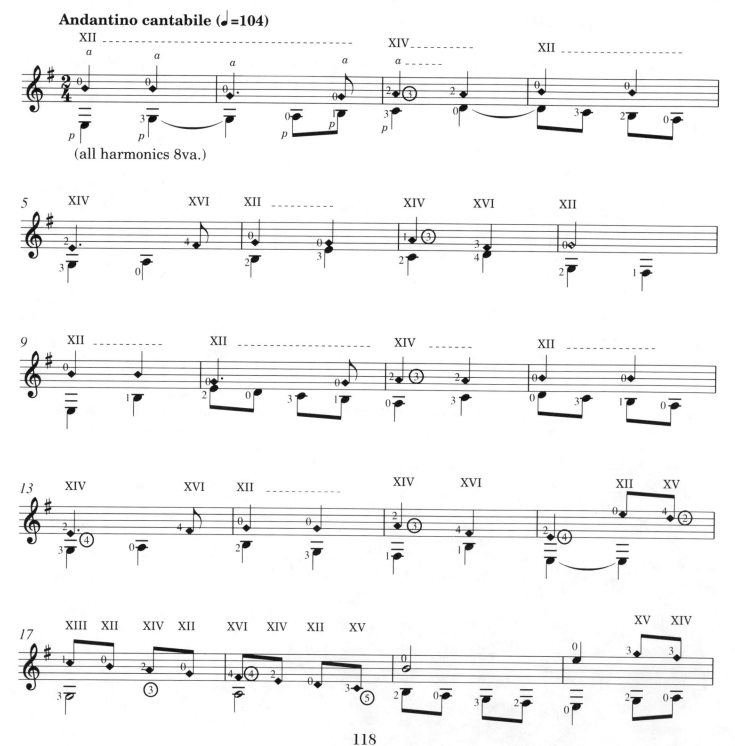

This composition is a *glosa* from a 16th century Villancico found in the book *Silva de Sirenas* by Enríquez Valderrábano (Valladolid, 1547).

LESSON 116

Fingering

328. — To complete the work of this course, the pupil will form the following three-note chords on the strings indicated, fingering them and writing them down himself, seeing that the distribution of the fingers is logical and correct. He should bear in mind the following remarks:

1st — The separation of more than one fret between adjacent fingers should be avoided for any chord whatsoever.

2nd — Provided the first string can be stopped with the index finger, the barré should be used when two or more notes are found at the same fret on different strings.

3rd — Provided that a given finger is common to two notes on the same string belonging to different consecutive chords, said notes are played with the same finger.

Exercise 245

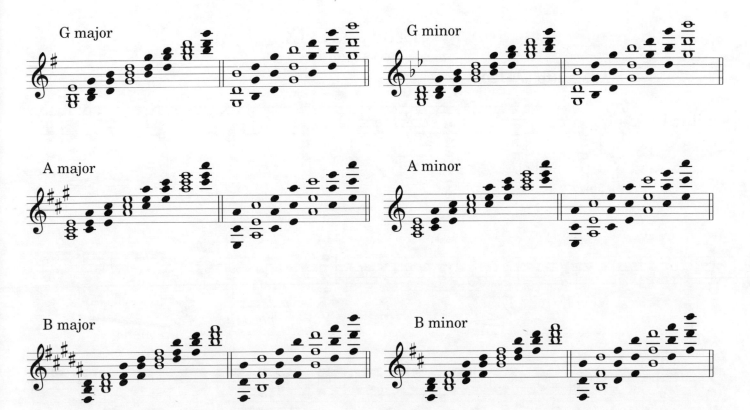

329. — On a separate piece of paper, write down the following chords and indicate to the left of each note the number corresponding to the finger used to stop it. Likewise, above those chords which require it, indicate the barré and fret where it must be used.

Specific Instructions for Study XXXIX

359. — With an end toward affirming a sense of ensemble and with it the discipline required to subordinate oneself while joining one sonorous element to another, we include this Study which, jointly with original and transcribed works by celebrated authors, will induce the studious pupil to indoctrinate himself in this aspect of vast instrumental illumination.

a) The chords whose notes are taken in by a bracket ([ ), should be played with a single stroke of the *thumb* having positioned itself at the lateral exterior edge of the hand over the strings next to the bridge so that, like a mute, it muffles the sound of the notes.

b) The passage for Guitar I from bar 27 to 32, inclusive, is, by its nature sympathetic to the Andalusian *falseta* and should be played with the fingers indicated, respecting the continuity and rhythmic accent of the melodic line.

360. — Since each of these Studies is a synthesis of a given aspect of technique, the pupil will be able to incorporate them into his daily practice throughout the course to which they belong, in substitution of the exercises they review.

361. — To practice the reading and performance of ensemble playing, the pupil will profit from the works for two guitars of Sor, Giuliani, Carulli, Ferdinand Rebay (Editions Musikverlag V. Hladky, Vienna), Fortea, and other authors whom the teacher will assign to the pupil according to his capabilities.

362. — Having mastered the studies in this course to which are added others by Sor, Aguado, Carcassi, Coste, Tárrega, Llobet, Fortea, and any others the teacher believes useful, the pupil will be in a position to form a basic repertoire of authors from the Classical, Romantic, and Modern authors whose difficulties are understood as a result of the problems which have been dealt with here.

Study XXXIX
for two guitars

Study XXXIX
for two guitars

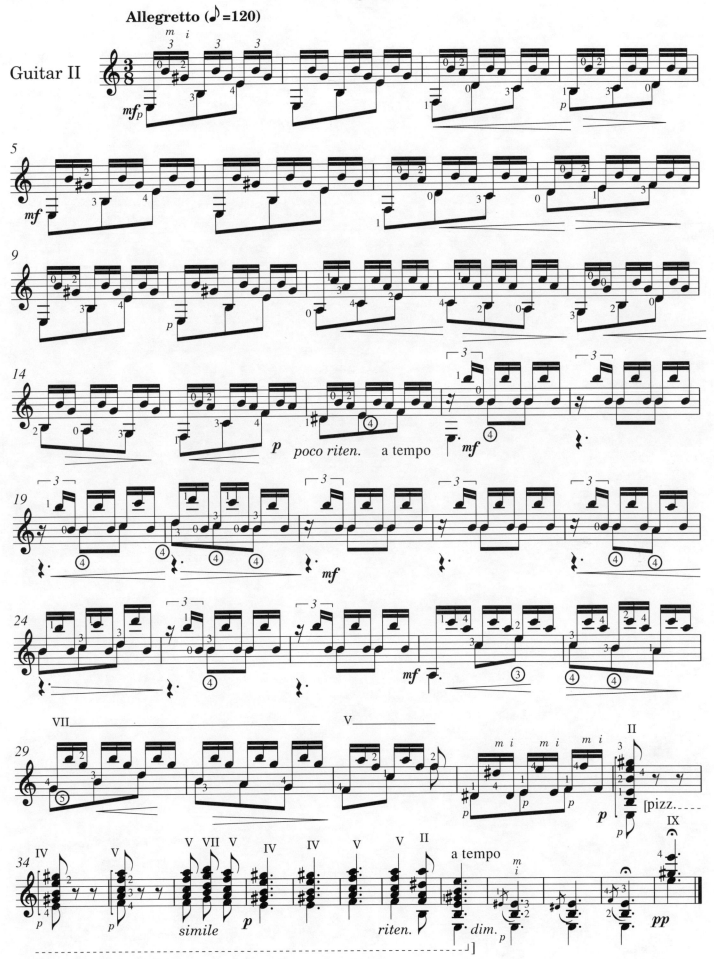

END OF BOOK III

This book was designed, edited and set at Editions Orphée, Columbus.
Cover design by Philidor Press, Boston. The text type is New Caledonia SemiBold.
Text was entered by Peter Segal in WordPerfect 5.1 software.
Music was engraved by Peter Segal in SCORE 3.0 software.
Final design and pagination was made by Matanya Ophee in VENTURA 3.0.
Linotron output provided by Dwight Yaeger Typographer, Columbus.
The Printing of this book was completed in October, 1991 at
McNaughton & Gunn Lithographers, Ann Arbor, Michigan.